Everett D. Hendricks, M.D.
1055 Ruth Street
Prescott, Arizona 86301
D0461155

FORT TRYON FOLIAGE FRAMING THE GEORGE WASHINGTON BRIDGE

THE NEW JERSEY PALISADES, 400 FEET ABOVE THE HUDSON RIVER

A SPRING SUNSET OVER THE HUMMOCKS OF JAMAICA BAY

CENTRAL PARK'S MEADOWS AND WOODLAND SHROUDED IN MORNING MIST

A PLANT-CHOKED STREAM IN A BRONX PARK

SNOW-CLAD BOULDERS ON A SLOPE ABOVE THE HUDSON

A RED-OAK FOREST ON STATEN ISLAND

RED-CEDAR SKELETONS AT DAWN ON SANDY HOOK BEACH

Everett D. Hendricks, M.D.
[illegible] Ruth Street
Prescott, Arizona 86301

Other Publications:

WORLD WAR II
THE GREAT CITIES
HOME REPAIR AND IMPROVEMENT
THE WORLD'S WILD PLACES
THE TIME-LIFE LIBRARY OF BOATING
HUMAN BEHAVIOR
THE ART OF SEWING
THE OLD WEST
THE EMERGENCE OF MAN
THE TIME-LIFE ENCYCLOPEDIA OF GARDENING
LIFE LIBRARY OF PHOTOGRAPHY
THIS FABULOUS CENTURY
FOODS OF THE WORLD
TIME-LIFE LIBRARY OF AMERICA
TIME-LIFE LIBRARY OF ART
GREAT AGES OF MAN
LIFE SCIENCE LIBRARY
THE LIFE HISTORY OF THE UNITED STATES
TIME READING PROGRAM
LIFE NATURE LIBRARY
LIFE WORLD LIBRARY
FAMILY LIBRARY:
HOW THINGS WORK IN YOUR HOME
THE TIME-LIFE BOOK OF THE FAMILY CAR
THE TIME-LIFE FAMILY LEGAL GUIDE
THE TIME-LIFE BOOK OF FAMILY FINANCE

URBAN WILDS

THE AMERICAN WILDERNESS/TIME-LIFE BOOKS/ALEXANDRIA, VIRGINIA

BY OGDEN TANNER

AND THE EDITORS OF TIME-LIFE BOOKS

Time-Life Books Inc.
is a wholly owned subsidiary of
TIME INCORPORATED

FOUNDER: Henry R. Luce 1898-1967

Editor-in-Chief: Hedley Donovan
Chairman of the Board: Andrew Heiskell
President: James R. Shepley
Vice Chairman: Roy E. Larsen
Corporate Editor: Ralph Graves

TIME-LIFE BOOKS INC.
MANAGING EDITOR: Jerry Korn
Executive Editor: David Maness
Assistant Managing Editors: Dale Brown, Martin Mann
Art Director: Tom Suzuki
Chief of Research: David L. Harrison
Director of Photography: Melvin L. Scott
Senior Text Editors: William Frankel, Diana Hirsh
Assistant Art Director: Arnold C. Holeywell

CHAIRMAN: Joan D. Manley
President: John D. McSweeney
Executive Vice Presidents: Carl G. Jaeger (U.S. and Canada), David J. Walsh (International)
Vice President and Secretary: Paul R. Stewart
Treasurer and General Manager: John Steven Maxwell
Business Manager: Peter G. Barnes
Sales Director: John L. Canova
Public Relations Director: Nicholas Benton
Personnel Director: Beatrice T. Dobie
Production Director: Herbert Sorkin
Consumer Affairs Director: Carol Flaumenhaft

THE AMERICAN WILDERNESS
Editorial Staff for *Urban Wilds:*
EDITOR: Robert Morton
Text Editors: Marion Buhagiar, John Man, Rosalind Stubenberg
Picture Editor: Patricia Hunt
Designer: Charles Mikolaycak
Staff Writers: Sally Clark, Carol Clingan
Chief Researcher: Martha T. Goolrick
Researchers: Joan Chambers, Terry Drucker, Lea G. Gordon, Villette Harris, Beatrice Hsia, Kumait Jawdat, Trish Kiesewetter, Howard Lambert, Mary Carroll Marden, Suzanne Wittebort, Editha Yango
Design Assistant: Vincent Lewis

EDITORIAL PRODUCTION
Production Editor: Douglas B. Graham
Operations Manager: Gennaro C. Esposito
Assistant Production Editor: Feliciano Madrid
Quality Director: Robert L. Young
Assistant Quality Director: James J. Cox
Associate: Serafino J. Cambareri
Copy Staff: Susan B. Galloway (chief), Barbara Quarmby, Susan Tribich, Florence Keith, Celia Beattie
Picture Department: Dolores A. Littles, Joan T. Lynch
Traffic: Barbara Buzan

CORRESPONDENTS: Elisabeth Kraemer (Bonn); Margot Hapgood Dorothy Bacon (London); Susan Jonas, Lucy T. Voulgaris (New York); Maria Vincenza Aloisi, Josephine du Brusle (Paris); Ann Natanson (Rome). Valuable assistance was also provided by the following individuals: Sue Wymelenberg (Boston); John Petty (Houston); Carolyn T. Chubet (New York); Martha Green (San Francisco).

The Author: Ogden Tanner, a former editor for TIME-LIFE BOOKS, is the author of *New England Wilds* in The American Wilderness series and a contributor to other books on nature, science, gardening, history and photography. Born in New York City, he has been a feature writer for the *San Francisco Chronicle,* associate editor of *House & Home* and assistant managing editor of *Architectural Forum.* He acquired his interest in urban wilds through explorations of the unexpected natural riches in and around New York and other metropolitan areas.

The Cover: Within sighting distance of Manhattan, a stand of tall phragmites reeds gives a golden cast to the marshes of the Jamaica Bay Wildlife Refuge. This carefully protected wetland wilderness affords sanctuary to thousands of birds, like the stately white egret standing on the near shore and the gulls floating in the background.

© 1975 Time-Life Books Inc. All rights reserved. No part of this book may be reproduced in any form or by any electronic or mechanical means, including information storage and retrieval devices or systems, without prior written permission from the publisher, except that brief passages may be quoted for reviews.
Second printing. Revised 1977.
Published simultaneously in Canada.
Library of Congress catalogue card number 75-4116.

Contents

Pockets of Wilderness in the Metropolis

Though "urban wilderness" would seem to be a contradiction in terms, many an American city has within or around its borders one or more natural enclaves that fully fit the description. New York, the ultimate metropolis, contains a wealth of such wild places. They range in type from the salt marshes and ocean beaches of Long Island to the swamps of New Jersey and the forested highlands of the Hudson River Palisades. Small in extent and coexisting in perilous proximity to human habitats, they nevertheless preserve the pristine look of the land as effectively as any sprawling national park in the West.

On the map at right, parks and other reserves are represented by a dark green tint outlined in red; woodland tracts by a medium green; and suburban wetlands, fields and woods by a light green. Swamps and marshes are marked by blue dashes, rivers and streams by blue lines, and roads by numbered white lines. The yellow tint indicates virtually complete urban development.

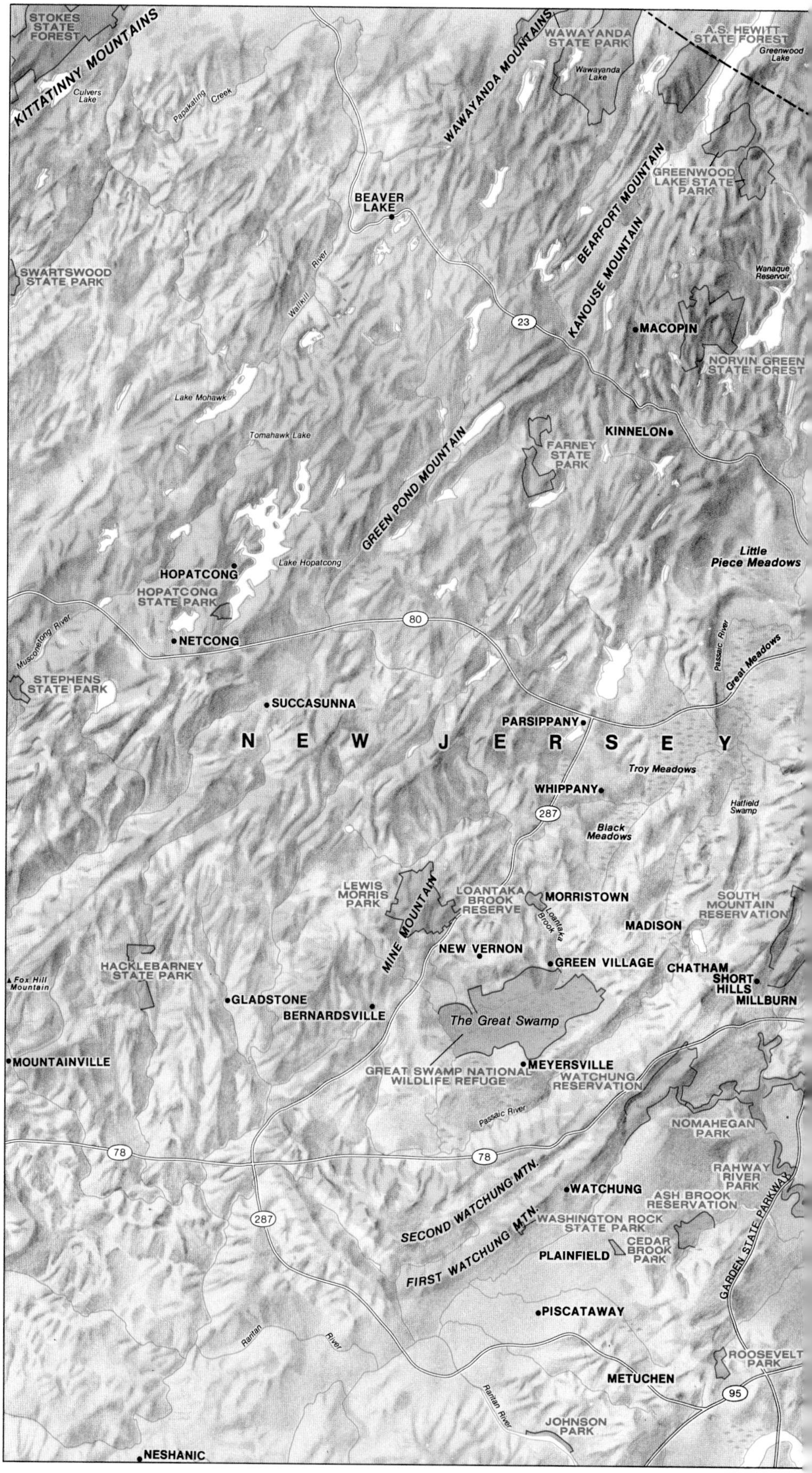

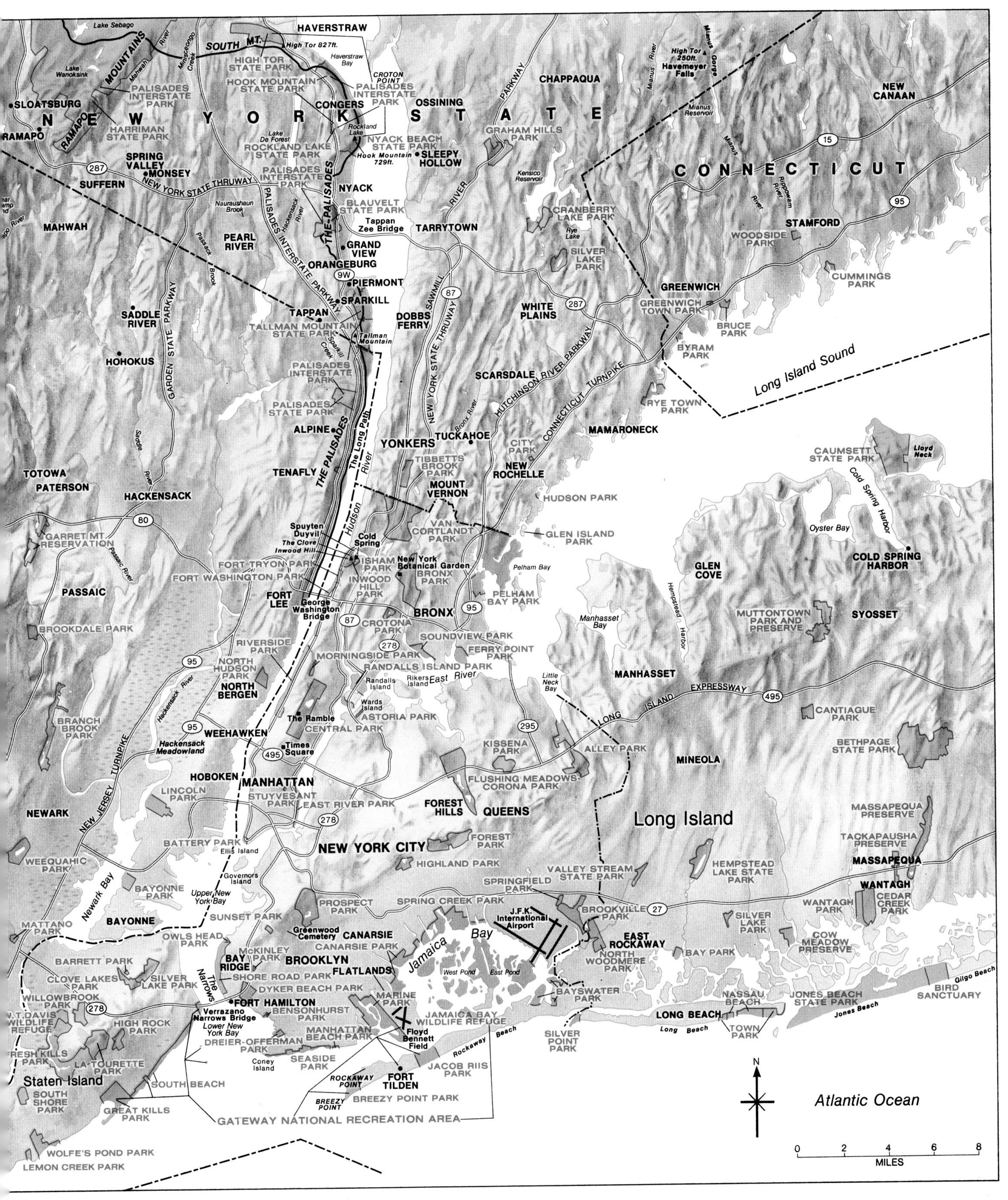

Lake Sebago
HAVERSTRAW
SOUTH MT.
High Tor 827ft.
Haverstraw Bay
Lake Wanoksink
MOUNTAINS
Mahwah
River
Minisceongo Creek
HIGH TOR STATE PARK
HOOK MOUNTAIN STATE PARK
CROTON POINT
PALISADES INTERSTATE PARK
PALISADES INTERSTATE PARK
CONGERS
OSSINING
CHAPPAQUA
PARKWAY
Mianus River
High Tor 250ft.
Havemeyer Falls
Mianus Gorge
NEW CANAAN
Mianus Reservoir
SLOATSBURG
N E W Y O R K S T A T E
RAMAPO
RAMAPO
HARRIMAN STATE PARK
Lake De Forest
Rockland Lake
ROCKLAND LAKE STATE PARK
NYACK BEACH STATE PARK
Hook Mountain 729ft.
SLEEPY HOLLOW
GRAHAM HILLS PARK
15
C O N N E C T I C U T
SPRING VALLEY
287
MONSEY
SUFFERN
NEW YORK STATE THRUWAY
PALISADES INTERSTATE PARK
NYACK
Kensico Reservoir
Mianus River
Rippowam River
95
MAHWAH
Nauraushaun Brook
Hackensack River
PALISADES INTERSTATE PARKWAY
THE PALISADES
BLAUVELT STATE PARK
Tappan Zee Bridge
TARRYTOWN
RIVER
CRANBERRY LAKE PARK
Rye Lake
STAMFORD
PEARL RIVER
Passack
Brook
GRAND VIEW
ORANGEBURG
9W
PIERMONT
SPARKILL
SILVER LAKE PARK
WOODSIDE PARK
CUMMINGS PARK
GREENWICH
SADDLE RIVER
GARDEN STATE PARKWAY
TAPPAN
TALLMAN MOUNTAIN STATE PARK
Tallman Mountain
Sparkill Creek
DOBBS FERRY
SAWMILL
87
WHITE PLAINS
287
GREENWICH TOWN PARK
BRUCE PARK
BYRAM PARK
HOHOKUS
PALISADES INTERSTATE PARK
NEW YORK STATE THRUWAY
SCARSDALE
HUTCHINSON RIVER PARKWAY
CONNECTICUT TURNPIKE
Long Island Sound
PALISADES STATE PARK
RYE TOWN PARK
Saddle River
ALPINE
Bronx River
TUCKAHOE
MAMARONECK
YONKERS
The Long Path
TIBBETTS BROOK PARK
CITY PARK
CAUMSETT STATE PARK
Lloyd Neck
TOTOWA
TENAFLY
THE PALISADES
River
NEW ROCHELLE
Cold Spring Harbor
PATERSON
MOUNT VERNON
HACKENSACK
HUDSON PARK
Hudson
80
Spuyten Duyvil
The Clove
Inwood Hill
Cold Spring
VAN CORTLANDT PARK
GLEN ISLAND PARK
Oyster Bay
GARRET MT. RESERVATION
Passaic River
FORT TRYON PARK
ISHAM PARK
New York Botanical Garden
BRONX PARK
Pelham Bay
GLEN COVE
COLD SPRING HARBOR
FORT WASHINGTON PARK
INWOOD HILL PARK
PASSAIC
FORT LEE
George Washington Bridge
PELHAM BAY PARK
Hempstead Harbor
95
BRONX
MUTTONTOWN PARK AND PRESERVE
SYOSSET
Manhasset Bay
BROOKDALE PARK
87
CROTONA PARK
SOUNDVIEW PARK
RIVERSIDE PARK
278
FERRY POINT PARK
95
NORTH HUDSON PARK
MORNINGSIDE PARK
RANDALLS ISLAND PARK
Randalls Island
Rikers Island
East River
Little Neck Bay
MANHASSET
Hackensack River
NORTH BERGEN
Wards Island
LONG ISLAND EXPRESSWAY
495
BRANCH BROOK PARK
The Ramble
ASTORIA PARK
CANTIAGUE PARK
95
WEEHAWKEN
CENTRAL PARK
295
Hackensack Meadowland
Times Square
495
KISSENA PARK
ALLEY PARK
BETHPAGE STATE PARK
MINEOLA
NEW JERSEY TURNPIKE
HOBOKEN
MANHATTAN
FLUSHING MEADOWS CORONA PARK
LINCOLN PARK
STUYVESANT PARK
EAST RIVER PARK
FOREST HILLS
QUEENS
NEWARK
278
Long Island
MASSAPEQUA PRESERVE
BATTERY PARK
Ellis Island
FOREST PARK
TACKAPAUSHA PRESERVE
NEW YORK CITY
WEEQUAHIC PARK
HIGHLAND PARK
VALLEY STREAM STATE PARK
HEMPSTEAD LAKE STATE PARK
MASSAPEQUA
Newark Bay
Governors Island
SPRINGFIELD PARK
WANTAGH
BAYONNE PARK
Upper New York Bay
PROSPECT PARK
SPRING CREEK PARK
J.F.K. International Airport
BROOKVILLE PARK
27
WANTAGH PARK
CEDAR CREEK PARK
BAYONNE
SUNSET PARK
SILVER LAKE PARK
MATTANO PARK
OWLS HEAD PARK
Greenwood Cemetery
CANARSIE
EAST ROCKAWAY
COW MEADOW PRESERVE
CANARSIE PARK
Jamaica Bay
McKINLEY PARK
BROOKLYN
BAY RIDGE
NORTH WOODMERE PARK
BAY PARK
BARRETT PARK
FLATLANDS
CLOVE LAKES PARK
SILVER LAKE PARK
The Narrows
SHORE ROAD PARK
West Pond
East Pond
Gilgo Beach
DYKER BEACH PARK
BAYSWATER PARK
BIRD SANCTUARY
WILLOWBROOK PARK
FORT HAMILTON
MARINE PARK
NASSAU BEACH
JONES BEACH STATE PARK
278
W.T. DAVIS WILDLIFE REFUGE
Verrazano Narrows Bridge
BENSONHURST PARK
JAMAICA BAY WILDLIFE REFUGE
LONG BEACH
Jones Beach
HIGH ROCK PARK
Lower New York Bay
MANHATTAN BEACH PARK
Floyd Bennett Field
Rockaway Beach
Long Beach
TOWN PARK
SILVER POINT PARK
FRESH KILLS PARK
DREIER-OFFERMAN PARK
Coney Island
SEASIDE PARK
LA-TOURETTE PARK
JACOB RIIS PARK
N
ROCKAWAY POINT
FORT TILDEN
Staten Island
SOUTH BEACH
Atlantic Ocean
SOUTH SHORE PARK
BREEZY POINT
BREEZY POINT PARK
GREAT KILLS PARK
GATEWAY NATIONAL RECREATION AREA
0 2 4 6 8
MILES
WOLFE'S POND PARK
LEMON CREEK PARK

1/ Nature's Improbable Precincts

In the years to come, man will be overwhelmingly a city animal. He will find nature in the city; or he will be in danger of not finding it at all.

AUGUST HECKSCHER/ *FORMER NEW YORK CITY COMMISSIONER OF PARKS*

There is a curious belief among urbanized Americans that they have to pack up the kids and travel several hundreds or thousands of miles to find out what nature is all about. There also seems to be a notion that wild animals are to be seen only in national parks, zoos or on television screens, and that all our mountain and forest scenery is in the Rockies or Alaska.

Not so. Even for a city dweller, nature is often no farther away than his own doorstep, staring him in the face. Almost every major urban concentration in America embraces surprising numbers of parks and wildlife preserves within and around its boundaries. But even more unexpected and refreshing are the unorganized scraps of nature that one can find in any metropolis: hilltops, woods, reservoirs, swamps, streams, abandoned canals and railroad rights of way. Even cemeteries. Together they provide a considerable degree of greenery, fresh air and an astonishing amount of wildlife—and visiting them has none of the do-or-die, once-in-a-lifetime aspect of going to Yosemite or the Okefenokee. They are simply there, right at hand, to be savored at any time.

Furthermore, the explorer of the urban wilds does not need much in the way of equipment. In fact, the survival gear is as modest as the rewards can be great: a pair of thick-soled shoes (or perhaps waders if you want to probe the swamps), a sandwich or chocolate bar stuffed into your pocket, a flask of water and a local guide book or map. No nylon tents or freeze-dried foods to worry about, no sodden sleeping bags or hidden rocks boring a hole in the small of your back. After less than a day's outing, you can return from the urban wilderness, triumphant, to a hot shower and your own bed.

Some city people, of course, are more fortunate than others: San Franciscans, for example. Whereas some cities have managed to make a thoroughly monotonous mess of their steel and concrete growth, San Francisco, mostly through luck, has better preserved its wilderness assets. Mainly this has been because nature is on the side of San Francisco, with its hills and sunshine and blowing fog, cradling its bay in a spectacular landscape of blue and green. So despite almost a doubling of the population of the metropolitan area in the last 25 years, it is still a magical place. When I lived there some years ago I sampled many of the city's small outdoor pleasures: wandering along the wharves to watch the gulls dip and soar; walking through groves of flowering crab apple and cherry in Golden Gate Park. On Sundays I would sometimes drive north across the Golden Gate Bridge, past Angel Island glittering like an emerald in the water, then up through canyons fragrant with bayberry to the awesome redwoods of Muir Woods. Farther up on the tortuous switchbacks of the coast highway, the whole Pacific would open out to view.

In California and elsewhere in the West, though, a mere half day's jaunt opens up some of the country's greatest concentrations of mountains, forests and parks. It is in the more easterly parts of America that the urban wilderness is more unexpected, more intriguing, for that is where the people are—and, by and large, that is where the vast federal preserves are not. Chicagoans, for example, have their Lake Michigan and the nearby Indiana Dunes. But they are also blessed with the less-known Cook County Forest Preserve, a 64,000-acre crescent of parks and woodlands that rings the city. These wild enclaves provide highly popular and convenient picnic grounds around their perimeters (Chicagoans are great picnickers) and contain some remarkably wild woods in their interiors, prowled by raccoons, pheasants and even beavers.

Cleveland is justly proud of its so-called Emerald Necklace of park roads on which are strung the green beads of natural preserves. Similar green belts of rivers, roads and parks thread around and through Philadelphia. The latter boasts the 8,200-acre Fairmount Park within the city limits, and New Jersey's vast Pine Barrens are less than an

The remnants of wilderness in and around American cities are as picturesque and diverse as many of the most remote parts of the continent. Not one of the wild enclaves shown here is more than 16 miles from a busy city; some are within city limits.

ARMAND BAYOU PARK, HOUSTON

TRILLIUM TRAIL, PITTSBURGH

STONE MOUNTAIN PARK, ATLANTA

PALOS PARK, CHICAGO

Everett D. Hendricks, M.D.
1055 Ruth Street
Prescott, Arizona 86301

INDIANA DUNES STATE PARK, GARY

ALPINE LAKE, SAN FRANCISCO

BALCH CANYON, MACLEAY PARK, PORTLAND

THEODORE ROOSEVELT ISLAND, WASHINGTON, D.C.

hour away. In Washington, D.C., there are lovely woodland walks in Rock Creek and Anacostia parks, as well as on Theodore Roosevelt Memorial Island in the Potomac right opposite downtown, and along the old towpath of the Chesapeake & Ohio Canal.

The biggest metropolitan area of them all, however, and the most intriguing in terms of urban wild places, is the vast complex of human habitation that centers on my home territory, New York. New York's best-known patch of greenery is, of course, Central Park, 840 acres in the middle of Manhattan. Reclaimed from a squatters' wasteland late in the 19th Century by two brilliant landscape designers, Frederick Law Olmsted and Calvert Vaux, it is the classic example of created countryside in the heart of the metropolis. Some of it has the look and feeling of being quite wild. But despite its wide variety of plant and animal life—including squirrels, rats, bats and rabbits—Central Park is to me a carefully tended garden in comparison with the places I want to show you.

These other areas, all within the city's boroughs or reachable in short rides by car, bus or railroad, are either largely pristine wildernesses—like New Jersey's Great Swamp—or places that have been touched by civilization but have reverted to wildness, like the forests and cliffs of the Palisades along the Hudson River's west bank, or Inwood Hill on Manhattan's northern tip, or Jamaica Bay Wildlife Refuge near John F. Kennedy International Airport. In all these places, the patterns of nature assert themselves with striking clarity. Forests reveal the natural succession of grasses, shrubs and trees; rocky outcroppings tell of ancient earth movements; lowlands bear the imprint of ice-age meltwater; and all are havens for indigenous and migrating wildlife. Even the built-up areas of the city itself can reveal natural patterns, where plants and animals have crept in to colonize odd corners of the concrete jungle. Some time ago, author-naturalist William Beebe trapped 11 minks along the Bronx River, and exchanged their raw pelts for a set of furs from a Fifth Avenue furrier. In the 1950s a deer got itself entangled in a subway turnstile near Pelham Bay Park, also in the Bronx. In the early hours of one April morning, two patrolmen in Manhattan's Washington Heights, sent to investigate a disturbance, found an opossum, normally a fairly timid creature, holding off nine alley cats (the opossum was rescued and sent to the ASPCA). At one Bronx cemetery, skunks often get into an open grave just before a funeral service, posing a delicate problem of removal for the staff. Recently someone discovered a fox spoor in Inwood Hill—the animal must have walked over the Henry Hudson Bridge from the Bronx. A flying squirrel has been sighted in a Riverdale backyard, and a six-point buck on Staten Island.

In addition to all this, however, the miniwildernesses of New York, perhaps to an even greater degree than those of other cities, have an unexpected emotional impact. It is the contiguity and contrast between the natural and the overcivilized that does it: you can stand in deep forest, your feet in years of leaf mold, your back against an ancient tree, and hear quite close the roar of parkway traffic. You can lean against the wind on a rocky bluff above the Hudson and see the apartment blocks marching incongruously along the opposite bank. You can watch a heron standing motionless and scarcely visible against a backdrop of marsh reeds, while the angular silhouette of the city rims your field of view. It always seems to me a special privilege in such settings to be able to sample the sights and sounds of the wilderness: an explosion of ducks from the surface of a pond, a riot of competing saplings on the floor of an adolescent forest, mist hanging hauntingly over swampland little changed in thousands of years.

Where shall I take you first to show you my own particularly treasured urban wilds? Perhaps to the edge of Pelham Bay, where a finger of land juts into Long Island Sound from the upper Bronx. Here great horned owls roost in winter and the intricately ribbed rocks and misplaced boulders reveal the extent of New England's ice-age glaciers. Or maybe to the swamp at Van Cortlandt Park a few miles inland, where you might see a muskrat or a Virginia rail, if your eyes are sharp. Or to the New York Botanical Garden in Bronx Park, where in the midst of a carefully tended setting, 40 acres of untouched hemlocks serve as a reminder of what the primeval woods were like before man decided to make things better.

Or to Inwood Hill.

You have probably never heard of Inwood Hill. Neither have most New Yorkers, despite the fact that it is Manhattan Island's second largest area of greenery. The miracle of Inwood Hill, however, is not its size (about 200 acres) but the fact that it exists at all—a high, improbable knob of forest at the northern end of the busiest, most built-up piece of real estate in the world. Here, tall native tulip trees—instead of buildings—scrape the sky. Yellow spicebush blooms aromatically and the glens are alive with the songs of warblers in spring. Here, despite the roar of an occasional jetliner overhead or the wink of a beer can underfoot, you can imagine yourself for an instant back in the lush land that greeted the first white settlers almost four centuries ago.

A friend of mine named Sid Horenstein lives in an apartment building right near Inwood Hill, and he regards the place with abiding wonder and pride. Sid is a college professor and a geologist with The American Museum of Natural History; on a spring or summer evening he takes a subway train to the last stop at 207th Street and Broadway, walks a couple of blocks west and before dinner has a stroll in Inwood Hill, which he regards as his backyard. He also likes to show it to other people—including his college geology students, a group of amateur rock hounds he has organized as the New York Paleontological Society, his young daughters and assorted acquaintances and friends.

Here, part of the most ancient bedrock of New York emerges in a great whaleback of dark gray and brown. For this reason, Sid uses Inwood Hill and its geological history as the starting point to brief his listeners about the evolution of New York's special mixture of rivers, lowlands and contorted rocks. I found his verbal gallop down the millennia an exhilarating way to begin a morning's walk with him and his rock-hound group—and an exciting way to add an extra dimension of understanding about the natural life that is a part of every city.

The narrow entrance to one of Manhattan's earliest known dwellings —a cave visited by Indian hunting parties over 1,000 years ago—opens onto a rocky slope in Inwood Hill Park. Three-foot-high mounds of oyster shells found nearby, and layers of ashes inside, indicate that the hunters returned to the cave many times.

We met at the base of the hill. Sid passed out mimeographed cutaway diagrams showing three groups of layered rock bending sinuously beneath our feet. "All these layers," Sid began with a flourish, "were sediments laid down half a billion to a billion years ago in tropical seas. The sediments, compacted into rock, were then subjected to tremendous heat and pressure, which contorted them into folds and raised them hundreds of feet high. Eons of subsequent erosion cut these peaks down to low, rounded hills. Inwood Hill is one. That part of the Bronx," he said, pointing north across the Harlem River, "is another. The edge of these ancient rocks is marked by the Hudson, which is a geological and chronological frontier. Over on the other side, the cliffs of the Palisades are volcanic in origin, and they were formed 250 million years after the rock we're standing on."

We leaped forward in time to the next great formative event, the ice age, which reached its fullest extent along Long Island about 20,000 years ago. "At that time," Sid said, "the spot we are standing on was covered by a blanket of ice *a thousand feet thick.*" (Pause for effect.) "The ice scraped the whole region clean and dumped its burden of rock ten miles south and east of here in a moraine that forms the backbone

of Long Island. At its front, the melting ice created a huge outwash plain swept by rivers flowing from its face. Jamaica Bay and the rest of the southern Long Island coast were part of it. And as the ice retreated some lowland areas became huge lakes of meltwater. The Great Swamp in New Jersey, only about thirty miles west, is the remains of one."

During the year, Manhattan's Central Park is home to an astonishing total of 200 bird species, the most colorful of which are the songbirds shown here on perches within the park. The birds' favorite haven is the Ramble, a hilly, wooded 26.3-acre plot in the south-central part of the green oasis.

With this final chronological leap, we set out to examine at close quarters what nature—with a few interruptions—had done with the particular mound of rock that is Inwood Hill.

"This is the famous Cold Spring," Sid announced, stopping to poke aside some dead leaves with a stick to reveal a meager trickle of water oozing from the ground. Famous? Well, not as famous as it deserves to be. Successive tribes of Indians used this place as a campsite for over 1,000 years, and the spring was its heart. The area where they camped was extensive. Sid led us up a short incline onto a hillock some 25 feet high and poked about with his stick again, exposing the white remains of oyster shells. We were standing on top of a huge, overgrown kitchen midden, a refuse heap on which generations of Indians had thrown the leavings of their meals. A few hundred feet farther up in a small declivity—called the Clove because it divides the rock mass of Inwood Hill like the notch in a cloven hoof—a jumble of slabs had slid from the cliff above to form several shallow caves. From the layers of ashes, stone tools and pottery shards unearthed in them, archeologists have concluded that these caves were the earliest known dwellings on Manhattan. Clearly, it had for centuries justified its later Indian name: Shora-Kap-Kok, "the sheltered, safe place."

It was not to be a safe place forever. In 1609 Henry Hudson, employed by the Dutch to seek out a northwest passage to the East, sailed his *Half Moon* up the river later named for him. On his way to what is now Albany he put in at Spuyten Duyvil, the inlet that branches off the Hudson and separates Manhattan Island from the Bronx mainland just above Inwood Hill. He was greeted by a canoeful of Weckquaesgeek Indians, and promptly captured two of them, probably intending to take them back to Europe as souvenirs of the trip. Both escaped; one drowned in the effort and the other swam back to camp. On Hudson's return from Albany, he put in at the same place again; three canoes of angered Weckquaesgeeks sallied forth with bows and arrows and were turned back by cannon and muskets, losing a half-dozen warriors before the *Half Moon* weighed anchor and sailed for home.

Fifteen years later the Dutch were back to build Fort Amsterdam at

TWO BOBOLINKS

WHITE-THROATED SPARROW

TUFTED TITMOUSE

BALTIMORE ORIOLE

YELLOW WARBLER

CAPE MAY WARBLER

BLACK-THROATED BLUE WARBLER

RED POLL

HERMIT THRUSH

MAGNOLIA WARBLER

MOCKINGBIRD

SCARLET TANAGER

the island's southern tip, and in 1626 Peter Minuit accomplished his celebrated purchase of Manhattan for $24 worth of goods. Some historians believe that this bargain may have been negotiated not at the fort but right near the Cold Spring at Inwood Hill. Apparently from the very start both Dutch and Indians interpreted the agreement somewhat differently, and there were frequent hostilities and bloody punitive expeditions until the Indians were finally forced out of Inwood Hill, their last stronghold on Manhattan, around 1715.

We climbed farther up the Clove, walking now between the stately shafts of tulip trees. These trees, which grow throughout the Eastern region and are among the tallest trees east of the Rockies, are a particular favorite of mine. At Inwood Hill the trunks, often measuring a good three feet through, rise 60 or 70 feet like Doric columns before even beginning to branch. The tree was much prized by the pioneers; its clear white wood made superb paneling and excellent canoes.

The name is somewhat misleading—the tulip tree is not related to the garden tulip, and is in fact the queen of the magnolia family. Nevertheless, the term is descriptive. The tree is tulip-like both in the outline of its leaves and in the general aspect of its flowers, whose greenish-yellow petals, splashed with orange at the base, twinkle high up in the branches like candles in the bright spring sun.

The tulip trees of Inwood Hill are among the oldest living things in New York; some have been alive for nearly 200 years. The onetime patriarch among them, measuring 20 feet around and 165 feet high, was sorrowfully removed by the Parks Department in 1938, a victim of age, decay and wind damage. Its age at the time was estimated at about 280 years. A commemorative plaque nearby records where it stood, near the old Indian camp, and notes nostalgically that the great tree had been the last living link with the area's former inhabitants.

Farther up the Clove, Sid pointed to a couple of strange-looking holes a foot or more across, exposed to view in the steep bedrock above the path; they looked as though they had been bored by a giant drill. They were, it turned out, exceptionally fine specimens of glacial potholes, carved by the cutting, grinding action of streamborne sand and gravel swirling beneath the melting ice.

Above them, part of the face had been almost totally split away from the bedrock; this slab was supported only by a single boulder, carried here by ice from the Palisades and lodged in this strange position when the ice retreated. A short distance beyond was another glacial memento, a *roche moutonnée*, or sheep-shaped rock. This outcrop, some 15 feet

Everett D. Hendricks, M.D.
1955 Ruth Street
Prescott, Arizona 86301

long, had been neatly ground smooth over its north-facing "head" and rounded "back" by iceborne rocks, and plucked ragged on its "tail" side as the ice moved over it.

Now we doubled back above the Clove, still climbing. Here on the heights, Dutch freeholders, who had moved in after the Indians had been dispossessed in the early 18th Century, came with ax and saw to take out firewood. In 1776 the high ground became key territory in the Revolutionary War. The British occupied it and by 1779 most of the forest had been cut down to keep the military campfires burning.

When the soldiers left in 1783, landowners returned and set about reclaiming the land. The hills grew green again and fine country homes were built on the heights. At the beginning of the 20th Century, with urban pressure mounting, this area became a target for land speculators. Some leading citizens issued a plea that this place, so rich in history and beauty, be salvaged by the city. In 1916, after much delay and debate, it was made a park. The estates were bought up and the houses razed, and nature was left to take its course.

Today, most of the man-made traces are gone. On the high ground only a stone retaining wall or the occasional outline of a foundation can be seen. Nonindigenous trees brought in by homeowners have merged gracefully with the native woodland species. Near the top of the hill, a few apple and cherry trees still blossom, and a lone Siberian crab apple stands almost overwhelmed by later growths of bramble. One insistent foreign species, however, successfully rivals the oak and beech: the sturdy ginkgo, which grew only in China until seedlings were imported by seekers after things fashionably Oriental, first to Europe, and then in the late 18th Century to America.

Finally we reached the summit of Inwood Hill, a wind-blown escarpment that overlooks the broad sweep of the Hudson. The river at this point is almost a mile wide. Beyond it the dull brown ramparts of the Palisades rise out of their spring greenery. It is a view that must have changed little since 1,000 years ago, when the early Indians made the place their home. We savored it, quietly, for several minutes. Then we turned, passed a jogger in a sweat suit and a couple out with their dog, and walked back down to the city in time for lunch.

The Inner Shapes of a Forest

PHOTOGRAPHS BY RALPH WEISS

Close to most urban centers in the United States flourish forests of surprising size and diversity. The one shown on these pages stands atop the Hudson Palisades near New York City. These urban woods are very different from the forests the colonists found. Plagues such as chestnut blight and Dutch elm disease have long since toppled enormous stands of indigenous trees; gypsy moth, sawfly and other insects have done their own destructive work. And by far the most destructive agent of all—man—has burned, cut and plowed virtually all the virgin woodlands.

Yet these remaining enclaves of second- and third-growth trees have a special fascination of their own that best reveals itself before the full bloom of leaves hides their intricate architecture. In addition to containing many examples of the original tree types, these woods play host to a greater number of species than do many less-disturbed forests: imports and invaders have colonized the open areas.

The Palisades contain more than two dozen major kinds of trees. In the thin soil on rocky ridges, hardy chestnut oaks thrust their roots down into the harsh seedbed. Where fires have cleared away broad areas of other growth, birches appear. On the lower hillsides, where the soil is deeper and the accumulation of decayed leaves holds more moisture, stands of hemlock mingle with hardwoods like red and white oak, sugar maple and hickory. The loamy, well-watered lowlands nourish willows as well as oaks and maples.

Within this variegated pattern one can discover a precise natural order: each tree grows not only in specific areas but generally in association with certain other species. And the trees succeed one another in a particular way. Thus, the light-seeking birch begins to die from lack of sunshine and nutrients as soon as competitors such as the oaks and sugar maples appear. The tough, shade-tolerant hemlock, on the other hand, grows steadily among its competitors until it triumphs almost totally over everything in the vicinity but such shade-loving trees as the beech. In a similar manner the tamarack, which appears here at the southernmost tip of its coastal range, dominates bogs and wet places.

Thus, in an endless cycle, old trees die and new trees spring up and grow to maturity as the forest inexorably regenerates itself.

The protruding nubs on this chestnut oak mark the loss of a number of branches, perhaps victims of fire or storm damage in this exposed, windy highland. Its fallen branches, like those of trees in the background, will decay on the ground among leaves and other debris and thus will help fertilize the growth of a new tree—possibly of a different species.

In the rich, well-watered soil at the base of a slope, young sugar maples and oaks flourish in close association. The deeply furrowed mature sugar maple in the foreground—perhaps a century old—contrasts with the pale, slender saplings that must compete with it for sunlight and soil nutrients.

The warping, curling plates of bark and gnarled limbs of this 70-foot giant identify it as a mature shagbark hickory, common to the Palisades. This hickory, distinctly North American, mixes with oak and other broadleaf trees on fertile soil, and produces a rich crop of nuts for woodland animals.

In response to some major injury —probably attack by insects or storms —that sheared off its crown, this 150-year-old sugar maple has sprouted a Medusa-headed tangle of younger limbs. Normally, sugar-maple branches grow in symmetrical pairs that extend from opposite sides of the trunk.

A slender gray birch less than 20 years old rises in a clearing. The sun-loving birch probably grew the jogs in its trunk as it bent to avoid the shade cast by neighbors. Vulnerable to the weight of ice and snow, the birch is relatively short-lived compared to such sturdy trees as the sugar maple.

European imports in the midst of the American forest, weeping willows grace the marshy banks of a Palisades pond. Willows require waterside habitats not only because of the plentiful sunlight in such open areas, but also to assure replacement of the huge quantities of water that their leaves give off as vapor. Willows colonize new soil as their twigs and seeds are carried off by river currents.

Everett D. Hendricks, M.D.
1?55 Ruth Street
Prescott, Arizona 86301

The dead and broken branches of a hemlock bristle from the trunk like a porcupine's spines. The hemlock casts such dense shade that it kills off not only its own lower branches but most other trees, forming a stable plant community called a climax forest.

Spindly, light-colored beech saplings, intermingled with slender oaks and maples, emerge against a dark stand of hemlock in the background. Beeches, which often cluster in thickets, are among the few trees that can live in the deep shade cast by hemlocks.

The tamarack, a conifer more often found in Canada, has invaded damp and marshy habitats in the Palisades. One of the few conifers that shed their needles in winter, the tamarack, like the hemlock, sometimes crowds out other species. Curiously, although the tamarack is adapted to a wide range of soil types, moisture and temperature, it can succeed only when it completely dominates, reaching into the overstory to capture the sun from its competitors and, in the process, creating a climax forest.

2/ Sanctuary on the Subway

A dawn wind stirs on the great marsh. With almost imperceptible slowness it rolls a bank of fog across the wide morass. Like the white ghost of a glacier the mists advance. . . . A single silence hangs from horizon to horizon. ALDO LEOPOLD/ *A SAND COUNTY ALMANAC*

However many times I do it, I still find that arriving in New York by air after a spell away is an awesome experience. As the airplane skims in over Long Island, I find myself overtaken by the city's pulsing power and sheer size. Beneath me the urban landscape unrolls: endless suburban plots, drab apartment blocks, cemeteries, row houses, the snaking arteries of expressways pumping the city's traffic back and forth. To the west I glimpse the gleaming towers of Manhattan and, in the hazy distance, the industrial sprawl of New Jersey. Such is the fascination of the sight that for years it obscured a fundamental fact about New York, one that is obvious from the air: it is a city set in water, a city of islands and rivers, of inlets and spits, of tidal flats and marshes, with an infinity of intricate edges where river and sea meet the land.

It would be nice to say that all these edges are still as beautiful as they once were. They are not. Most of the close-in waterfronts are hidden behind aging piers, warehouses, oil terminals and docks. Others have been obscured under rising mountains of garbage—for marshland, long considered expendable, has been the traditional place for the city dump. Still other waterfronts have been preempted for expressways and airports, or taken over by housing developers.

But as the plane sweeps around for its final descent into Kennedy Airport, there comes a sudden reminder that the urban matrix is not all embracing. You find yourself above a marshy, semicircular lagoon almost eight miles long by four miles wide, crisscrossed by meandering channels and dotted with green islands where little but cordgrass and tall phragmites reeds wave in the wind. This area, nearly the size of Manhattan Island and crossed by only one road and a rapid-transit line, is one of New York's most prized possessions—Jamaica Bay.

Jamaica Bay is a classic combination of man-made and natural wilderness. It has been described in many superlatives: the largest wildlife refuge within the boundaries of any city in the world; a signal environmental success in a city that can boast all too few; a unique sanctuary on the subway where one can see glossy ibis, snowy egret and more than 300 other species of birds. It is all of these, and thus has become something of a rallying point for the preservers of the fast-disappearing wetlands all along the Atlantic Coast.

Although for most wilderness lovers the birds are the main attraction of the area, for me the bay's great appeal resides in its mysterious, brooding beauty and distant horizons. Jamaica Bay always induces in me a feeling of timelessness. I start to ponder those ancient events without which the birds, the refuge, the bay and indeed New York itself would not exist. When I go out there, I sometimes take along a sandwich lunch and sit for a while on one of the rustic benches spotted along the main bird-watching path. Looking out over the marshes and tidal inlets, I try to visualize early stages of this landscape, when it was so much more imposing than the city that borders it today.

Looking northwest, where the Empire State Building and the twin towers of the World Trade Center rise on the skyline through a faint brown smog, I turn the clock back 17,000 years and imagine the vast blanket of ice that, moving southward, covered the spot where these tallest of skyscrapers now stand. The front of the glacier, straddling what is now Brooklyn and Queens, stretches away east along Long Island and west through Staten Island. It is the edge of the last great ice sheet, stalled athwart New York, where its rate of advance has been matched by its rate of melting.

I picture the front as a huge, shining, blue-white cliff, packed with the debris the ice has picked up as it scoured the land to the north; as the front melts, dropping its burden, more ice continually moves up from behind. From time to time I see great blocks of frozen material the size of apartment buildings break off from the mother pack, loosening with an eerie creaking before they slide thunderously down to smash into mere house-sized chunks below. Gushing from the face of the glacier toward and around me are hundreds of meltwater streams carrying boulders, pebbles and sand to form an immense and barren outwash plain. Behind me the plain stretches 100 miles to the sea, which lies more than 300 feet lower than today, its moisture locked up in the earth's hugely expanded ice cap.

Now, a few hundred years pass in my mind's eye and the climate warms enough so that the stalemated ice front begins to retreat at last. Its farthest line of advance is marked by a bumpy terminal ridge of detritus 200 or 300 feet high. Today this ridge, which geologists call the Harbor Hill Moraine, rises across Staten Island, jumps the Narrows and continues across the center of Brooklyn and Queens as the high ground of Fort Hamilton, Bay Ridge and Forest Hills.

As more of the great ice cap melts I picture the sea rising, century by century, gradually drowning the coastal plain. It flows into a huge inland lake trapped behind the glacial moraine. Called Lake Flushing, this body of water will eventually form Long Island Sound. At the same time, the land, released from its burden of ice, rises until Lake Flushing and other meltwater lakes to the west spill over and cut down through the moraine to form the present-day Narrows at the mouth of the Hudson. As the sea rises, currents sweep sand westward from the tip of prehistoric Long Island. The sand forms a succession of streamer-like barrier beaches, the last of which now make up the south shore: Southampton and Westhampton beaches, Great South Beach, Jones Beach, Long Beach and then Rockaway Beach, lying behind me now, separating Jamaica Bay from the sea.

Tall stalks of tough, flowering cordgrass rise from the mud flats of Jamaica Bay. A single plant of this prolific tidewater species, once it gains a foothold, multiplies by sending out fresh growth from its roots, eventually forming entire islands of grass.

In Jamaica Bay itself the sea formed a unique horseshoe-shaped inlet, drowning what some geologists believe to be the remnants of a shallow, preglacial river valley. Over the years, sediment built up in the bay to form tidal flats—the foundations of today's necklaces of low green islands. These green patches, like those in the other tidal marshes that fringe Long Island, New Jersey, Connecticut and the rest of the Eastern coastline, are made up largely of two grasses: *Spartina alterniflora,* a coarse, tough plant, can live with its roots in salt water much of the time; *Spartina patens,* a smaller variety, thrives in drier areas.

These grasses are the keys to the marsh life of Jamaica Bay. They bind together the rich sediments washed down toward the sea by upland streams, and the sand washed in by the sea. Generations of dead stalks pile up to form peat that—along with the algae and plankton flourishing in the tidal pools—nourishes billions of tiny organisms.

These organisms, in turn, nourish increasingly larger ones in the food chain, including snails, mussels, clams and oysters, crabs, small fish, muskrats, voles, and thousands of shore and water birds. This food chain has existed for centuries—and the time inevitably arrived when it attracted one more predator on its pinnacle: the human animal.

The region's early inhabitants, the Canarsie and Rockaway Indians, lived well on the bay's finned fish, shellfish, waterfowl and an occasional basking seal. The ample provender also appealed to the early Dutch colonists, who established their first settlement on Long Island in 1634 on the western border of Jamaica Bay at Flatlands. To the Dutch, and to the English who soon followed them to the vicinity of the "Rockaway Swampe," the marshes were invaluable not only as hunting and fishing grounds but also for the grasses that grew there. The coarsest spartina, cordgrass, was used as roofing thatch; the grass of shallow waters was dried and banked against houses as insulation during winter; and the tenderer, smaller spartina variety was harvested from higher land as salt hay. The settlers' cattle seemed to prefer salt hay to all other fodder, at least until the seeds of their "English hay" could be planted in sufficient quantities on upland farms. As I look out across the marshes, I can almost see the salt hay scythed and raked into neat stacks that dot the meadows, curing in the sun for the winter ahead.

As late as the 1880s Jamaica Bay remained a bountiful and largely untrammeled place. By then, though, the city's gridiron patterns were marching out toward it, sending their sewage and garbage ahead. A branch of the Long Island Railroad, built on a wooden trestle across the center of the lagoon, carried vacationers out to the fashionable new seaside resorts that had sprung up along the sands of the Rockaways. In 1915 a scheme was proposed to dredge the entire bay and transform it into a vast industrial port larger than the harbors of Liverpool, Hamburg and Rotterdam combined; the proponents of the idea chartered a ship and toured the ports of Europe to advertise the glories of "Jamaica Harbor," the new colossus of the world. Nothing came of the venture, however, and the single pier that had been built at Canarsie for big oceangoing vessels remained the sole expression of the dream, today a place where fishermen cast their lines for flounder or striped bass.

In the meantime a little community of stilt houses called Broad Channel had grown up on an island bisected by the railroad trestle; during Prohibition it flourished for a time as a center for nightclubs, yachting parties and the rum-running trade and was nicknamed Little Cuba. By the 1930s some of the other islands had become sites for fishermen's and squatters' shacks, including a picturesque collection of jerry-built houses that artists often came out to sketch.

Around this time, the bay became the focus of a battle between developers and protectors. In 1931 New York's first airport, Floyd Bennett Field, was created on the bay's west side. The critical moment in the confrontation between exploiters and preservers came when the Commissioner of Sanitation proposed to use the bay as the next city dump. New York City's Parks Commissioner, Robert Moses, retaliated with a hard-fought propaganda campaign and in 1938 secured the bay as a protected area under his control. The last great incursion came in 1948, when Idlewild (later Kennedy) Airport was built on 4,500 acres across the northeast curve of the bay.

For the bay's protectors, a major advance came in the early 1950s. The old railroad trestle was badly damaged by fire. The Transit Authority proposed to take over the line from the Long Island Railroad, and dredge sand for a new embankment on which to run subway trains out to the now heavily settled Rockaways. Moses granted permission for this on one condition: that the transit people, while they were dredging, build him two circles of dikes that would gradually fill up as a pair of large fresh-water ponds to attract a variety of birds. Out in the lagoon to the west he also arranged to have the rich sludge from a sewage treatment plant piped out to an island named Canarsie Pol. Worked into the bare sand, the sludge made it fertile enough to support plant life for nesting shore birds. As for the fishermen's and squatters' shacks, Moses decreed they would have to go.

In 1953, the New York City Parks Department established the Jamaica Bay Wildlife Refuge. It got off to a fine start, for its first superintendent was Herbert Johnson, a Parks Department employee who devoted his native ingenuity, and 20 subsequent years of his life, to turning the refuge into the unique sanctuary that it is today.

When Herb Johnson arrived for work his first day on the job, the prospects looked singularly bleak. He was not a trained wildlife manager; he had worked in an experimental nursery and studied golf-course grasses at a soil-testing laboratory in the Bronx. But he had learned a good deal about plants from his father, the superintendent on a large Long Island estate, and he had earned a degree in applied horticulture on his own. Though he knew virtually nothing about birds, he started reading books about them, talking to ornithologists and visiting other wildlife refuges.

Backed by New York City's built-up Rockaway shoreline, migratory water birds pause to feed in Jamaica Bay on their spring trip north.

The first thing Johnson did was to have 1,550,000 individual clumps of beach grass transplanted onto the dikes to hold the newly dredged sand before it blew away. As the two ponds encircled by the dikes filled with water from rain and snow, turning the sea water increasingly fresh, he planted a few aquatic species favored by ducks, geese and coots: sago pondweed and widgeon grass in the 40-acre West Pond, muskgrass in the 100-acre East Pond. During the winter he encouraged the ducks that stayed around by throwing out corn and seed and chopping holes in the ice to keep patches of water open.

Despite water pollution and the noise of the nearby aircraft, waterfowl had never quite deserted Jamaica Bay, and they responded to Johnson's efforts by coming back in increasing numbers. But he wanted to make the refuge attractive to land birds as well, and began looking into the kinds of trees and shrubs that they liked. He had noticed that autumn olive, which thrived in the harsh, salty conditions along shore parkways around the city, was favored by many birds, so he propagated some of his own from cuttings gathered here and there. Its plump pink berries provided food for some 40 different species, including the robin, mockingbird, starling, brown thrasher, red-winged blackbird and grackle. In similar fashion he set out clumps of wild rugosa and multiflora roses, which yielded tasty orange-red rose hips in late summer; he also planted red and black chokeberry, Russian olive, beach plum, American holly and bayberry, whose waxy fruits proved special favorites of swallows, warblers and quail. Johnson wanted to put in Japanese black pines as hardy winter cover, but his budget did not permit him to buy them. So he collected their cones from a nearby park in Queens, extracted and planted the seeds at the refuge, and nursed them along until they were tall enough to transplant. They soon began to offer shelter and nesting sites as well as seeds for winter finches, and roosting sites for saw-whet and horned owls.

The results were impressive. The bay began to develop a new ecological richness. With the additional food and cover provided by thicker vegetation, squirrels, mice and rabbits thrived. With luck, you could even see an occasional muskrat. But the real success story was that of the birds. Where perhaps 60 species of birds might have been seen during a typical year before the refuge was established, in five years the total had grown to 208. The count nowadays is over 300, including some 250 species that are more or less regulars and 50 or 60 that are rarities or "accidentals." These latter sightings can cause great excitement

Everett D. Hendricks, M.D.
1055 Ruth Street
Prescott, Arizona 86301

in New York bird-watching circles. In February 1959, a little European red-winged thrush, not known to have visited North America before, brought to the bay swarms of binocular- and notebook-toting birders —including a group of Texans who, in proper Texas fashion, chartered a plane to come up and add the species to their life lists. A similar flurry occurred in October 1964, when a big white pelican, which normally migrates from the Northwest to the Gulf Coast, was blown far off course and stopped in for a rest on its way south.

One of the most reliable attractions at the refuge became the large number of water birds that adopted the place as their summer breeding grounds: snowy egrets, common egrets, blue and green herons, least bitterns, common gallinules, pied-billed grebes, ruddy and black ducks, shovelers and blue- and green-winged teals. In late summer and fall the larger and less-visited East Pond became a likely place to spot the shier visitors like avocet, long-billed dowitchers and Wilson's phalarope, and the whole refuge teemed with waterfowl, migrant land birds, and shore birds like gulls, herons and terns. In winter, the grassy summer nesting grounds abandoned by the terns were frequented by short-eared owls, Lapland longspurs, snow buntings and Ipswich sparrows. And in spring as well as fall, the activity grew to spectacular proportions, for the bay is a major stopover on the Atlantic flyway that funnels snow geese, Canada geese and many others on their way back and forth from nesting grounds across the northern continent to winter quarters in the south.

One of the bay's biggest single success stories is the return of the glossy ibis and the snowy egret. Because of its lovely white plumage, greatly prized in the 19th Century for ladies' hats, the elegant, long-necked egret had been hunted almost to extinction by the early 1900s. Its plight played a major role in the formation in 1896 of the Massachusetts Audubon Society, the forerunner of today's national bird-protection group. The society's members began an extended campaign to persuade fashionable women to abandon their addiction to egret feathers. They succeeded: by the 1930s the egret was making its comeback. In 1960 two pairs were observed nesting at Jamaica Bay; 15 years later between 50 and 75 pairs regularly made it their summer home.

An even more exciting comeback to some ornithologists is that of the glossy ibis, formerly found almost exclusively in the south. In the early 19th Century, there had been occasional sightings in the New York area of this graceful, long-legged wader with its reddish-brown plumage and downcurved bill, but until the mid-20th Century none had been seen for almost 100 years. Then, in 1959, one was sighted in the refuge, and two years later three nests containing eggs were found. No one knows why the birds came back—perhaps it was the result of population pressure in their home territory, or a small climatic change that made the north acceptable. In any event, the number of nesting pairs has steadily increased until in recent years up to 100 have sometimes been counted in the refuge.

A cottontail peers from thick grasses at the edge of Jamaica Bay Wildlife Refuge. Seldom seen in the refuge as recently as the 1950s, cottontails have come back strongly due to increased greenery, but are still prey to hawks, owls, disease—and dogs and cats.

One sunny spring Saturday I joined a local Audubon group for an outing at the bay. The parking lot was already half full when we arrived, and other groups and families were milling about, limbering up binoculars, spotting scopes and long-lens cameras. As we started out through a grove of Japanese black pines, our leader, a knowledgeable amateur ornithologist named Ted Barry, pointed out a yellow-shafted flicker in the branches, a gorgeously variegated bird with speckled black and white breast, red-patched nape, black collar and "mustache." In flight it becomes a veritable explosion of color with its yellow wing linings and white rump flashing in the sun. On another branch a mourning dove brooded impassively, apparently aware that she was in safe territory even when we approached to a distance of three or four feet.

As the grove opened out to the path along the low, broad dike surrounding West Pond, a bobwhite sounded from the brush, and high in a tree a long-tailed brown thrasher sang its varied, mimicking song, repeating each phrase (like its cousin the mockingbird) in case you hadn't caught it the first time. Red-breasted robins and shiny purple grackles poked around in a grassy spot for insects and worms, and from somewhere in the thicket came the plaintive melody of a white-throated sparrow. We strolled farther out onto the dike. The pond was alive with dabbling ducks and coots, and we looked out over the mud flats exposed by the tide.

"Clapper rail!" Ted called crisply. "Right over there beyond that swampy area, walking from right to left." Nearby three snowy egrets were exploring the watery marsh for a meal, and a flight of glossy ibis winged over the lagoon. Other terse announcements came at intervals as someone made a new find: "Seaside sparrow, down in the grass there somewhere. Hear him?" "House finch, over there."

Pencils jabbed busily at check lists. "Norma has a life list of 596," one woman confided to another, a little gloatingly, "and she *missed* the seaside sparrow!" On a sandy spit we could see a crowd of black-headed laughing gulls walking about and chuckling to themselves; overhead four gadwalls spun around in what someone described as a

courtship flight. A flock of Canada geese in their familiar V formation wheeled up gracefully against the sun.

One of my companions, I noticed, had his eyes fixed firmly on the ground and was absorbed in loudly kissing his thumb, whistling and making other strange sounds to attract some warblers or sparrows close enough for identification. When they failed to respond, he chalked them off as "LBBJs" (Little Bitty Brown Jobs, he explained, a term used for any small birds that look alike or that you are not skillful enough to tell apart). As we continued around the dike we made easier identification of a killdeer as it zipped in front of us, its zebra stripes flashing, repeating its name in a clear voice. Down in the marsh we spotted black-bellied plovers, a black-crowned night heron and a trio of handsome drake shovelers.

By now little knots of birders were strung out on most of the two-mile-long path, dressed in everything from bandannas and battle jackets to floppy hats and hiking boots. One family—a mother, father and two teen-age girls, all resplendent in bright red sweat shirts—were engrossed in a clump of bushes trying to entice a bobwhite into the open by whistling its name. Wandering from group to group was a large, bespectacled man wearing an old camouflage suit and hat, with a large Styrofoam hawk decoy dangling from one hand, a gunstock-mounted camera with a 400-millimeter lens cradled in the other, a pair of immense binoculars around his neck and a live magpie jumping around on his shoulder.

I struck up a conversation with him, and as we talked I learned that his name was John Bode (known as Cheyenne Bode although he came from Long Island). His pet magpie's name was Shoo-Fly-Pie. Bode told me he worked mostly as an artist and photographer, painting pictures of birds and giving illustrated lectures to local groups. Jamaica Bay, he said, was still one of his favorite places. You could find most things from hummingbirds to eagles here; one of the latter, a young bald eagle, turned up at the bay regularly for a while and was promptly named the Brooklyn Daily Eagle—in fond if inaccurate memory of the borough's now-defunct newspaper, the *Brooklyn Eagle*.

There were also two goshawks that visited over the winter, he said; they were named Killer and Son of Killer, and cold-weather regulars at the bay watched with fascination as they seized smaller birds on the wing. Cheyenne also pointed out several flocks of brant, which to me looked like sawed-off Canada geese. He noted that they had been making quite a comeback. They had become very scarce in the 1930s when a parasite destroyed large areas of eel grass, their favorite food; but they had since learned to eat the marine algae called sea lettuce.

In the near distance the big jets of Kennedy ("gashawks," Herb Johnson used to call them) made their ponderous way into the sky. How all the birds of Jamaica Bay managed to coexist with the noisy human flyway that drones over them, I thought, has to be a matter of no small wonder in itself. Apparently they have adapted to the urban din like other New York residents, whether they like it or not. They keep largely out of the bigger birds' way, and airline officials have never been too concerned about their posing a hazard to flight operations. The main threat has been to the birds, from oil and gasoline washed into the bay and from the possibility that new runways may be built to handle mounting traffic volume, thus nibbling away still more of the bay. Recently, however, the refuge has acquired some high-level political clout. In 1974, the National Park Service took it over as part of the Gateway National Recreation Area, a group of New York area parks and preserves, including some military posts that are being phased out. To build anything in Jamaica Bay now takes an Act of Congress.

It is a matter of deep satisfaction to Herb Johnson, who took a well-earned retirement in 1972, that his life's work is secure. And appreciated: about 100,000 people visit the bay every year. Among them are groups of amateur and professional ornithologists from all over the world. More important to Herb Johnson, however, is the way Jamaica Bay has introduced bird watching, conservation and nature in general to fellow New Yorkers. Among these are the thousands of city-bred and city-bound schoolchildren for whom the bay, now a valued teaching asset, has added a whole new dimension of experience—a glimpse of wings and water, of beautiful wildness, only a subway ride from the crowded city's core.

Birds of the Urban Shore

In many American cities the most conspicuous, and sometimes also the most numerous, of the wild creatures are shore birds. Raucous killdeer by the tens of thousands cruise along Chicago's lake shore. Surfbirds and dowitchers—cousins of the snipe—throng the edges of San Francisco Bay. New Orleans plays host to dense flocks of yellowlegs and least sandpipers. And, as the pictures at right and on the following pages illustrate, the waters around New York's Long Island provide a hostelry for dozens of species, among them egrets, ibises, skimmers and stately Canada geese.

For the birds, these urban areas were familiar camping grounds for eons before the first building ever went up in America. Most shore birds tend to be migrators, heading south for the winter and returning north in the spring to breed—sometimes covering as much as 14,000 miles in the round trip. Like human travelers, they need places to rest and feed along the way. Their choice of stopovers depends in large part on their habitual flight paths.

North American migratory birds travel along four aerial highroads known as flyways. Two of these flyways follow the Atlantic and Pacific coasts; a third sweeps across the Mississippi and Missouri river valleys; and the fourth covers Great Salt Lake, the scattered smaller lakes of the Great Plains and the Gulf of Mexico.

As cities grew along these routes the avian migrants saw no need to change their flight course. And today, despite the crush of urban development, the birds do very well indeed. They find shelter in reeds and grasses and dunes that fringe the shoreline. Both land and water provide plentiful sources of food. And when the time comes to lift off for destinations as far north as the arctic tundra or as far south as the Argentine pampas, the transients have experienced a full measure of urban hospitality, enough to ensure their return another day.

Some migratory birds, in fact, have decided that the city is not just a nice place to visit, but that it is a fine place to stay. Emulating such permanent residents as the herring gull, more and more migrants have been settling in for nesting and breeding. Since birds usually return, when mature, to the scene of their birth, the lake, river and coastal cities of America provide rich dividends for urban wildlife watchers.

Canada geese, back from a winter in warmer climes, ride the waters of a New York City inlet on a chill February day. First of the springtime migrants to appear, they may tarry for several weeks, feeding mainly on marsh grasses before they fly on to their breeding grounds farther north.

A Rich Harvest in the Shallows

For water birds, the food pickings are lush along New York's shoreline. Vegetation, insects, frogs, crustaceans, small fish and minnows are the favored fare. Shallows close to shore—notably those near the protected areas of Jamaica Bay Wildlife Refuge and Jones Beach State Park—are popular browsing grounds, where each bird species brings into play its own special skills at foraging and hunting.

Some species, such as ducks, swim about in search of prey, paddling with webbed feet on the surface; submerged, they use their wings as flippers. Other water birds hunt on the wing: a gull may swoop down to the surface when it sights a victim, snatch it from the water in mid-flap and return skyward in one graceful arc; a tern plunges into the water from a high dive, sometimes submerging completely; the aptly named skimmer hunts in shallow tidal flats, flying a mere inch or so above the water with its lower jaw just below the surface *(right)*.

A third hunting style, slower and more deliberate but no less effective, is favored by such wading birds as the heron and its relative the egret. Stalking through the shallows of the New York coastline on their spindly legs, they will find a likely larder, stop, brace themselves on the mucky bottom, and wait, immobile. Then, with a sudden movement of their flexible necks, they will reach down and nab the prize.

Herring gulls use the vantage point of a sand spit to scout for tidbits of food in the

A black skimmer cruises at the water's surface, dipping its bill for morsels.

surrounding waters. Voracious and aggressive, they will eat almost anything—not excluding the eggs and tiny chicks of other water birds.

Tallest of the wading birds, a four-foot-high great blue heron hunkers down for the kill during a fishing foray at the edge of a salt marsh.

A snowy egret takes off for an after-dinner flight at the Jamaica Bay refuge. Once nearly killed off for its coveted plumes, the species has made a remarkable comeback at the refuge: its numbers have grown from two nesting pairs in 1960 to a whole colony today.

An American egret preens itself in the shallows off New York's south shore. In so doing, the bird distributes a glandular secretion that waterproofs the feathers and repels pollutants, such as gasoline and oil from passing barges —provided the spill is not too heavy.

Everett D. Hendricks, M.D.
1055 Ruth Street
Prescott, Arizona 86301

Snowy egrets and glossy ibises inspect the housing possibilities of the dense shrubbery along the south shore of suburban Long Island.

Tranquil Places for Nesting and Breeding

A bird's selection of a site in which to nest and produce its young represents a vote of confidence in its surroundings. The species that have chosen the New York area seem to be not a bit daunted by car-choked expressways or the march of high-rise apartments. Increasingly, shore birds that used to pause briefly in transit now stay on for months to raise their families. Rookeries of egrets, for example, are more numerous than ever; nesting by the glossy ibis, a rare tropical visitor until the 1960s, is no longer uncommon.

Around New York, many shore birds have chosen to settle where they have also found good feeding—Jamaica Bay Wildlife Refuge and Jones Beach State Park. Nest building reaches its peak in May, signaled by intensive searches for a cozy spot and a flurry of collecting reeds, twigs, seaweed and waterborne debris. Some birds, such as the heron and the ibis, construct their homes aloft, in bushes and trees, while others prefer to stay at or near ground level. The common tern, for instance, seeking a suitable place to deposit its eggs, simply sweeps out a shallow depression with its beak in a fine-grained sandy beach.

A nest is either a solitary affair or in a colony of perhaps thousands. Once settled, the parents go about brooding their eggs—and then the seemingly endless chore of stuffing food into the mouths of voracious chicks *(overleaf)*.

A little blue heron mother feeds her chicks in a protective stand of shrubbery at Jones Beach.

A common tern and its hungry hatchlings (above) use the sands of Jones Beach—summer haunt of swarms of city dwellers—as a nesting site.

A downy herring-gull chick (below) seeks its mother's cool shadow. Like the adults, young gulls learn to scavenge food scraps left by bathers.

Back from the hunt, a laughing gull flaps down to its brood in a south-shore marsh.

On a crisp September day that heralds the beginning of the fall migration, snow geese take off from Jamaica Bay for their wintering grounds along Chesapeake Bay and the North Carolina coast. Of all species that use New York as a stopover on their journey from the far north, snow geese usually stay the shortest time—a mere 24 hours, unless delayed by a storm.

3/ Ramparts of the City

I gazed with wonder and admiration at cliffs impending far above me, crowned with forests, with eagles sailing and screaming around them. WASHINGTON IRVING/ 1851

Of the hills and valleys that fan out west and north of New York City across Bergen, Rockland and Westchester counties, the single richest vein runs up the west bank of the Hudson. Here, the river sets off the grandest scenery of highlands and headlands to grace the doorstep of any metropolis I know. I refer, of course, to the Palisades, the irregular line of high, igneous-rock cliffs that run 45 miles along the river, rising out of the ground at Staten Island, curtaining the Hudson up past the George Washington Bridge and petering out inland after a final flourish at High Tor near Haverstraw. The lower stretch of the cliffs south of the bridge has been largely obscured by factories, ship terminals and neon signs, and by glassy apartment towers that stand brazenly in front, or on top, of the battlements. But the northern two thirds, with a few commercial interruptions, have been preserved as a chain of nature-*cum*-recreation areas known collectively as Palisades Interstate Park (it actually extends beyond the Palisades area proper to include the 51,000-acre Bear Mountain-Harriman State Park).

I have known the Palisades for years, but to gain a more intimate acquaintance I took two trips, one in summer to immerse myself in the forest and see its supporting cliff-buttresses, and another in fall to the towering, open heights of Hook Mountain, to watch the area's most dramatic wildlife spectacle: the annual migration of hawks.

One July day I set out to explore the section immediately north of the George Washington Bridge. Here the Palisades resemble most closely the structure after which they were named, for the rock rears up in cliffs that look like a colonial stockade of upended logs. I wanted to know about those cliffs, and I had little trouble persuading my geologist friend Sid to come along. About seven miles north of the bridge, near a lovely old stone mansion that now serves as the park's local headquarters, we parked our car. As we headed north into the woods, the rising heat of a muggy morning quickly evaporated in the cooling shade, and the sound of the parkway traffic died until it was no more than a breeze rising in mountain treetops or the washing of waves by the sea.

Like all forests in the region, the one on top of the Palisades has been cut over many times in the past, but it usually takes a forester's eye to tell, so diligently has nature healed its wounds with a wealth of different trees: oaks, maples, hickories, beeches, dogwoods, sassafras, sweet gums and occasional big hemlocks and tulip trees. In their shade were thickets of mapleleaf viburnum, carpets of Canada mayflower, ferns, Virginia creeper and the berry spikes of false Solomon's-seal. At every break in the woodland canopy, sun-loving vines sprouted in dense profusion—poison ivy, wild grape, wild raspberry, greenbrier—and staghorn sumacs raised their wine-red, military plumes of berry clusters above fuzzy branches and frondlike leaves.

As the path began to curve toward the cliffs, we noticed an inconspicuous side trail and set off down it to explore. It led to a small footbridge that had lost its railings; we crossed it over a fissure some 15 feet wide and 20 or 30 feet deep. We were now standing on Grey Crag, a sliver 10 to 20 feet wide and 300 feet long that had been increasingly isolated from its parent body by erosion. "Tons of rock fall off these cliffs every year," Sid observed lightly. "When this one goes, it will probably slump four or five hundred feet to the base of the cliff, then split up and take off in various directions, some of the chunks landing in the river. Should be quite a show." I pulled back from my vertiginous inspection of the edge, trying to ignore a tightening sensation in my stomach. "When do you think it will go?" I asked casually, sidling back toward the bridge. "Oh, any time," Sid replied with a smile. "Could go today, or maybe not until fifty years from now."

We resumed our walk, and Sid filled me in on the fine points, erosional and otherwise, of the Palisades. I had had a vague notion that these cliffs were the front of a great tidal wave of fiery lava that rumbled and burbled across the landscape a few million years ago, freezing instantly at the brink of the Hudson. Not so simple, I discovered. The

Palisades began some 190 million years ago as an oozing of molten rock into sediments that had been eroded from long-vanished mountains and tilted toward the west by later upliftings of the land. Some sizable sheets of lava spilled out on the surface to form the wavelike basalt ridges of the Watchung Mountains to the west. The molten material that was to form the Palisades, however, never reached the surface. It solidified underground, forming a broad horizontal tongue of igneous rock about 1,000 feet thick, which shrank and cracked as it cooled into the polygonal shafts that characterize the cliffs today. Erosion has since stripped off the overlying sediments and cut away the leading edge to create the ancestral Palisades.

On the western slope, by the way, some of the sedimentary rocks can still be seen and in a few places they contain fine fossil deposits. One find, made in 1960, has a particular fascination: in an abandoned quarry at North Bergen, a young man named Alfred Siefker and two fellow high-school students uncovered a small, odd-looking fossil, which they took to The American Museum of Natural History. There a paleontologist exposed the fragile bones of a lizard whose ribs extended out beyond the six-inch-long body. He concluded that these must have been covered by membranes to allow the creature to glide from tree to tree. The flying lizard—promptly named *Icarosaurus siefkeri* after its discoverer and the mythological Greek bird-man Icarus—caused a flurry of excitement. It was the first-known vertebrate to achieve flight, a few million years before the first winged reptiles.

This deep vertical fissure in the basalt escarpment of the Hudson Palisades was created underground almost 200 million years ago, when the molten rock underlying the area cooled and shrank. Eventually exposed by erosion and glacial scouring, the narrow crevice runs 500 feet from top to bottom.

As we rounded a promontory called Bombay Hook, we came to the highest spot in this section of the cliffs, Ruckman Point, which rises 520 feet above the river. Here, sitting on a bare ledge, with the river glinting in the bright summer sun like a sheet of crinkled tin foil beneath us, we had a fine view of the irregular rock faces that undulated off to the north. I could readily see how the Palisades got their name (the Indians saw the resemblance, too, and called the Palisades Weehawken, "the rocks that look like trees").

All along the cliffs, bits of rock have fallen away to form silhouettes that have been likened to the faces of Indians, Dutch patroons and crag-browed pioneers. From the river's edge, rocky mounds of this debris, or talus, slope upward, sometimes reaching an angle of 45° and obscuring as much as two thirds of the vertical face. Up the rubble have marched armies of shrubs and trees, finding footholds everywhere between the boulders; some hardy scouts have almost gained the top of

1055 Street
Prescott, 86301

the battlements, clinging in improbable crevices wherever their roots can take hold. The trees, it is evident, are helping to break down their own habitat, their roots powerfully seeking and expanding, adding to the forces of rain and ice that gradually pry loose the rock.

It was easy to see why the great bluffs have always seemed so impressive, and why they have come to be so zealously protected. The Palisades first attracted the admiring attention of white men in 1524, when the Florentine navigator Giovanni da Verrazano, sailing in the French ship *Dauphine,* entered the river's mouth. So struck was he by the dramatic beauty of the west bank that he described the whole region around New York as *la terre de l'anormée berge*—"the land of the great scarp"—a designation slightly altered by Mercator to Anorumbega in an early map. In 1609 the English navigator Hudson was impressed by what he called The Great River of the Mountains.

For over 250 years, settlers left the area largely alone except for lumbering in the forests. Then, in the second half of the 19th Century, wealthy men began to build rural retreats on the Palisades and quarrymen began their own brand of erosion, mining the rock to pave streets and sidewalks as well as to supply broken-stone aggregate for concrete roads, buildings, jetties and piers. By the turn of the century the river echoed daily to the sound of dynamite as one piece of cliff after another toppled in clouds of gray dust.

In response to public outcry against this defacement, the New York and New Jersey legislatures appealed to Congress to save the Palisades, suggesting they be made a military preserve. Congress declined, seeing little value in the cliffs for training troops. At this point, however, a far more powerful force came into play: a wrathful legion of ladies in high-button shoes. In 1900, the New Jersey Federation of Women's Clubs sponsored legislation that resulted in the creation of a Palisades Interstate Park Commission. When the new commission tried to buy out the worst offender—a large quarry north of Fort Lee where 12,000 cubic yards of rock were being blown loose every day—it found itself short of funds. George Perkins, one of the commissioners, turned to his friend J. P. Morgan the elder, who promptly donated $122,500 to complete the sale.

This was the first of a long and painstaking series of acquisitions and gifts involving 147 separate parcels of real estate along the New Jersey frontage alone. But with the repeated support of Morgans, Rockefellers, Perkinses and other prominent families, supplemented by public appropriations, a total of 75,500 acres up and down the Hudson was

A showy yellow spring flower adorns an eastern prickly-pear cactus. The only cactus found in the Northeast, this species—also called the Indian fig—produces a pulpy but edible fruit after its flowers die in early autumn.

eventually secured. In a clearing near the cliff edge we came upon a plaque and a tiny, turreted replica of a castle, erected to the memory of the women who had saved the Palisades "for the glory of God who created them and the ennobling of the generations which may henceforth enjoy them."

By such miracles, I thought as we walked, is the urban wilderness created—rescued from near disasters and assembled from used land. Indeed, the path we were now following toward the cliff edge was once a private road on a modest estate. The woods alongside revealed domestic plantings that had long since gone back to the wild: flowering rhododendrons, patches of shiny-leafed myrtle, delicate Japanese maples thrusting up incongruously among native beeches and oaks.

The trail wound back and forth down the forested face of the cliffs. At the bottom we emerged into an overgrown field by an abandoned boat landing, where the high grass fairly sparkled with color: the brilliant-orange flowering sprays of butterfly-weed, the fragrant, dusty-rose blossoms of milkweed, the violet-gray star bursts of wild onion and, nearer the water, purple loosestrife with its gaily blazing spikes. At the forest's edge, lush thickets of wild raspberries were ripening to a dark, glistening burgundy in the summer sun. Busily transferring the berries to a brimming pail was a man in shorts and an old baseball cap, a retired telephone company employee who told us he made the long climb down and up again almost every day during the berry season. We picked a few handfuls of the fruit ourselves, and it made a tart, delicious refreshment.

Along the shore a few hundred yards away, the path wound over a huge avalanche, and we clambered over rocks the size of automobiles that lay where they had tumbled into the water. High above we could see the scar of lighter-colored rock from which this gigantic load of debris had been ripped away. Sid pointed out a chunk of rock that had more recently tumbled down, splitting in half; its cleaved surfaces displayed a handsome salt-and-pepper pattern—the "bluestone" used for paving blocks. It is only after years of exposure to the air that the iron-bearing minerals in the rock oxidize to give the cliffs and rubble their characteristic reddish-yellow look.

I had heard of an ancient Indian campsite along this part of the Palisades shore, one of many up and down the Hudson, where archeologists have made intriguing finds. After consulting a sketch map we had brought along, we found a likely looking side trail, followed it for a while, then doubled back to a flat place in the forest about 100 feet above the river. Almost by accident we stumbled on the site, marked by low mounds of earth sprinkled with oyster shells, which had been excavated some years before. We poked around, half hoping to find something the excavators had overlooked—an arrowhead, grinding stone or pottery shard—but the rich collection, which included nearly 600 weapon points, had, of course, been carefully removed. From one large projectile point of flint, the diggers concluded that the site had been used as long as 7,000 or 8,000 years ago by aboriginal hunter-fishermen who had probably wandered north along the coast in their canoes. Later points, plus many bones and shells, indicated that local Indians had camped here intermittently beginning about 5,000 years ago, probably lured by the Hudson's huge runs of sturgeon, shad and bass, by the giant oysters (up to eight inches long) that once abounded in the river, and by the elk, deer and smaller game that inhabited its banks.

A frozen waterfall preserves the pattern of a stream's descent over a rocky abutment on New Jersey's Palisades. When spring thaws the ice, the stream's waters will move on to mingle with those of the Hudson River.

It looked to us like a snug enough place for a campsite, especially if you could send your squaw down to the river whenever you wanted some more fresh oysters on the half shell, not to mention lobsters, mussels and hardshell clams. Unhappily, such feasts are no more, and not just because of overharvesting or pollution; the natural process of silting has steadily reduced the tidal flow of salt water in the estuary, and the lower Hudson, now insufficiently brackish, produces only a few small oysters. I picked up an old shell from the midden as a memento of the Indian who ate its contents a few thousand years ago, and we began the long walk back to our car.

For my visit to Hook Mountain 15 miles to the north, I had to wait a full two months, when the hawk migration would be at its height. It is an ideal place for hawk spotting, directly on the eastern flyway from Canada and 729 feet above the water; over 11,000 birds have been counted from its summit in a three-month period. In this respect it is a smaller edition of Hawk Mountain, the celebrated sanctuary about 140 miles west of New York in the Pennsylvania Appalachians, whose rocky summit is aswarm with spotters during the fall migrations, and where between 25,000 and 30,000 birds of various raptorial species are sighted every year. Hook Mountain, however, has the advantage of being just 25 miles from Central Park and, along with places like the Montclair Hawk Lookout Sanctuary in New Jersey and Mount Peter in New York's Orange County, is far handier for hawk-minded city folk. A considerable rivalry exists between the watchers at Hook, Montclair

and Mount Peter, and sometimes modest bets are placed on the total number of hawks each group sights on a given day.

I set out one Sunday in mid-September, and arrived at the summit around noon. There were already some 30 or 40 people there, decked out with binoculars and perched expectantly on the rocks. "So far 419 hawks," a man in tweeds and a Tyrolean hat announced by way of a greeting. "A little slow right now. Should warm up later. There's a nice place for a picnic just over the crest, if you get hungry." I scanned the sky myself a few times, looking as professional as possible, but picked up only a DC-10 and an olive-drab helicopter. Clearly, I had some time. I found a grassy patch among the rocks overlooking the river and settled down in the sun for an early lunch.

From this pinnacle, I could survey almost 15 miles of the Hudson. The early Dutch skippers called the Hook Mountain ridge Verdrietige Hoeck—troublesome point—for as they sailed the river they were never sure whether they would have to look at this landmark for hours in a maddening calm or be suddenly set upon by some perverse wind. They would certainly have received little help from the current, for here the river broadens out to its widest point between the Adirondacks and the ocean—three and a half miles at Haverstraw Bay—and looks less like a river than a great blue inland sea.

A broad-winged hawk soars easily and majestically above the Hudson Highlands a few miles northwest of New York City. Unlike their larger cousins the falcons, which are stronger fliers, broadwings must rely on thermals along mountains like those west of the city to assist them in their long, twice-yearly migrations.

Toward its south end this broad expanse of water is still known as the Tappan Zee, a name that recalls both the Indians who once inhabited the area and the Dutch settlers who must have been reminded of their own Zuider Zee. To the south beyond the Tappan Zee Bridge, which links the Hudson's shores, I could make out a long thin line of trees that seemed to march out halfway across the water. They mark an overgrown pier of rock and earth built out over the Piermont Marsh in prebridge days to act as a terminus for the Erie Railroad and for one of the numerous ferries that plied the Hudson.

Feeding into the marsh at Piermont is a minor river, the Sparkill, which has an interesting history of its own. Sloping up from its banks is a broad, rounded gap in the Palisades, a gap that seems too wide to have been cut by such a modest stream. Geologists have pieced this incongruity together with other evidence to suggest that the Hudson, in one of several courses taken by the river in the last 70 million years, once ran westward through the Sparkill Gap, crossing and recrossing the Watchung Mountains farther inland in New Jersey before veering back again to meet the sea south of Staten Island at Raritan Bay. They believe that headwaters of a smaller river, roughly following the lower course of the present Hudson, ate their way north until the secondary stream finally "captured" the larger ancestral river and diverted its course to the one we know today.

Across the river from Piermont and Sparkill I could pick out other landmarks. To my left, separating the Tappan Zee from Haverstraw Bay, lay the low, broad hook of Croton Point, a reminder of the time when the old Croton River poured silt into a lake created when the Hudson was temporarily blocked behind the long ice-age moraine. Beyond Haverstraw Bay, I could just make out the southern gateway to the Hudson Highlands, where the river narrows and takes a sharp left behind a mountain called Dunderberg.

This is the beginning of the Hudson Gorge, a deep, fast-flowing, 15-mile stretch that is the northernmost, and one of the most productive, spawning grounds of the striped bass on the Atlantic Coast. The tens of thousands of striper addicts who ply the coasts of New York and New England may not realize it, but the fish they so devoutly seek probably started life in the Hudson, in the area from Haverstraw Bay north through the gorge. In a sense the same can be said for the fishermen on the California and Oregon coasts, for the striped bass they now enjoy in such quantities are not West Coast natives, but descendants of transplanted Hudson stock. It has been estimated that between 15 and 20 million stripers, in various stages of their lives, inhabit the Hudson at any one time. To preserve the breeding grounds, conservationists have opposed for years the building of a huge generating plant near the northern end of the Hudson Gorge at Storm King Mountain.

I discovered another cause for conservationist concern on this Palisades ramble, a rare and endangered plant whose presence here amazed me. The plant, which I discovered quite by accident, is the prickly-pear cactus, with its gorgeous yellow summer flowers, flat green pads, a few long spikes and deceptively innocent flabby points. I knew it, of course, to be a resident of the Southwestern desert and was surprised to learn —from the botanist who pleaded with me not to reveal its whereabouts —that a species has been native throughout the East from Massachusetts to Georgia for millions of years. Although widespread, it has apparently never been very abundant and is endangered for several reasons. First of all, it has been cleared out of many places where its barbed spines make it a nuisance. Second, it flourishes only where its requirement for well-drained soil and an open, sunny location is met; such sites have been increasingly hemmed in, built over or cleared for people. Finally, despite its prickly nature, it has been widely collected as a house plant by horticulturists who know how easy it is to propagate and maintain, and by florists who capitalize on its rarity. As a result, it is now on an official list of endangered native plants put out by the New York State Department of Environmental Protection—and on my own private list of natural phenomena whose specific whereabouts, in this case, I do indeed plan to keep secret.

Having finished my lunch, I climbed back to the bald knob of the summit where the crowd of bird watchers waited expectantly. In their midst was a lean, white-haired gentleman named Stiles Thomas, the official counter at this observation post for the Hawk Migration Association of North America, which was attempting to gather data from a whole network of lookouts to gain a better understanding of hawk migratory patterns and population trends. Thomas was slumped purposefully in a folding aluminum chair, binoculars held skyward in one hand and a mechanical counter poised in the other.

"Here they come!" someone yelled. "Due north, right up there in the blue patch between the clouds." Straining into my binoculars, my eyes managed to pick up one black speck, then another, then a dozen more, then more than I could count, heading steadily toward us from some invisible production line in the sky. "My God, it's the Luftwaffe!" exclaimed a man beside me in an awed voice. On they came—400, 500, 600 hawks in a single aerial armada, and still no end in sight. "I'm going to win that dollar bet with Mount Peter," Thomas said gleefully, punching away, "if this counter doesn't melt in my hand." The little band of bird watchers broke into a wild, impromptu cheer.

The oncoming cloud consisted entirely of broad-winged hawks, a shy woodland predator that is seldom seen except during migration, when it is easily recognized by its gregarious tendencies, its broad, chunky wings and the black-and-white banding on its fan-shaped tail. As they neared the mountain, their leaders began to drift into huge ascending circles that were joined by more and more birds behind, until the flight resembled a tornado in slow motion. This is one of the great sights that hawk watchers climb mountains for—a "kettle," or "boil," of broadwings churning in the warm air of a thermal, riding it upward for thousands of feet.

Near the top of the spiral, where the rising mass of air began to dissipate, the hawks peeled off like airplanes in formation, and with scarcely a flap of wings started a long, fast, flat glide toward the next thermal down the line, where they would form another kettle and ride it aloft. This kettle-and-glide flight pattern, peculiar to the broadwing, serves as a sociable and effort-saving way of traveling on long migratory flights, which range from summer nesting grounds as far north as central Alberta in Canada to wintering spots as distant as South America. On occasion the migratory groups take on the proportions of a wave: broadwing flights tracked by ground observers, radar and airplanes across New England and New York have taken as long as an hour and a half to pass a given point; at an average speed of 30 miles an hour such flights have been estimated at 45 miles in length, with the crest of the wave up to 10 miles wide.

Our wave was hardly of such dimensions, but in eight hours the counter had nevertheless clocked a total of 1,703 birds—905 of them in the single kettle of broadwings between 1 and 2 p.m. Almost all the rest of the birds we saw were broadwings, too, save for a handful of marsh hawks, sharpshins and ospreys. "The record for Hook Mountain is 2,903 hawks in one day," Stiles Thomas observed. "We have a couple of bottles of champagne buried here on the summit. The day we go over 3,000, we dig them out."

We were not to break the record that day, for the hawks seemed to have vanished as spectacularly as they had appeared. We sat for a while longer in the sun, occasionally scanning the sky. But it remained empty. Chairs were folded, knapsacks slung, and a line of pilgrims set off down the trail. No champagne this time, but the experience was worth a beer or two.

NATURE WALK / Down the Mianus Gorge

PHOTOGRAPHS BY ROBERT WALCH

Below a quaintly remodeled mill in suburban New York's Westchester County lies a fascinating and anomalous stretch of pristine wilderness known as the Mianus Gorge. Nestled in the valley of the Mianus River —stream might be a more accurate word, since the Mianus in most places is less than 30 feet wide—the watery wilderness extends for two miles or so before submitting to domestication in a reservoir for the town of Greenwich, Connecticut.

The wild gorge can be walked in a leisurely two-and-a-half-hour round trip. But every time I go there I find one good reason or another to prolong the experience. For in the space of those two miles, the river becomes the centerpiece for some of the loveliest untamed scenery remaining in the region; including a magnificent grove of hemlocks, some of which are more than 100 feet tall and three centuries old; over 200 species of native woodland wild flowers; an upland forest bright with beeches and flowering dogwoods; and, toward the end of the trail, one of the prettiest sylvan waterfalls I have seen.

The Mianus Gorge remains what it is—an island of wilderness in a suburban sea—largely owing to the persistence of a local naturalist named Gloria Hollister Anable, who chanced on it with her husband one day in 1952. Struck by its primeval beauty, and concerned by the housing developments beginning to encroach upon it, the Anables talked to a few friends about doing something to save the gorge. The Nature Conservancy, founded in 1951 as a nonprofit organization financed by private contributions, consented to make the Mianus its first project. Donations poured in from garden clubs and individuals, and gradually 39 pieces of land along the river were acquired by purchase or gift. By early 1975, a total of 347 acres had been assembled: they are maintained by the Nature Conservancy as a botanical preserve and wildlife refuge.

One day in May, when the gorge was fresh with the first rain-washed burst of spring, photographer Bob Walch and I set out to sample its delights. Through a thicket of viburnum dotted by budding shadbush and alder, we glimpsed the Mianus racing merrily along, narrowing as it cut through the sloping hills. Along the trail the blossoms of red trilliums nodded sleepily above their beds of winter leaves.

Abundant in the moist woodlands, the trillium is even more exquisite

Everett D. Hendricks, M.D.
1055 Ruth Street
Prescott, Arizona 86301

than most flowers in its pure geometry. As the first element in its Latin name – *Trillium erectum* – suggests, the plant's parts are symmetrical in threes: three petals, three leaflike sepals protruding beneath the petals, and below these a whorled trinity of leaves. As for the species name,

A RED TRILLIUM

erectum, it is derived from the firmly upright stalk–though more often than not the flowers themselves modestly hang their heads.

The red trillium has been known by a variety of other names: squawflower and birthroot (Indians decocted and drank it as a medicinal potion to aid in the labor stages of childbirth), red benjamin, wet-dog trillium and nosebleed. It is also variously called stinking willie because its odor is foul to humans (though apparently not to the carrion flies that

THE MIANUS RIVER ABOVE THE GORGE

SKUNK CABBAGE AND FIDDLEHEADS IN A FERN GLEN

pollinate it) and wake-robin, a more appealing celebration of the time of year of its flowering.

As we followed the trail a little farther along, it dipped across one of the Mianus' tributary brooks. Other early spring-blooming plants fairly filled a swampy glen. Here skunk cabbage formed a great emerald blanket. Called skunk cabbage not because the animal eats it but for its pungent smell and its resemblance to the garden vegetable, it appears before any other plant. These had long since pushed through the remnant patches of ice and snow that lingered, and now spread their floppy leaves in rosettes almost three feet across. Nearby rose a slender relative of the skunk cabbage, jack-in-the-pulpit. Its graceful spathe was arched above the upright spadix; this was the pulpited "preacher" that would later turn into a cluster of gleaming carmine berries.

A Fairyland of Ferns

Here and there were the tiny white flowers of miterwort and foamflower and the fragile star bursts of dwarf ginseng. And everywhere the fuzzy fiddleheads of young ferns stood like rolled-up party snappers waiting to be blown. Botanists who have catalogued the preserve have found no fewer than 27 species of ferns there, ranging from cinnamon, sensitive and maidenhair to New York fern, named for the area where it was first identified. There is also the tall, evergreen Christmas fern, so called because it is able to survive the December frost and because its lustrous jade leaves look to many people like tiny Christmas stockings.

CINNAMON-FERN FIDDLEHEADS

MARSH MARIGOLDS

WHITE TRILLIUMS

Clumped in watery spots amid the ferns and skunk cabbages were masses of marsh marigolds, whose bright canary blossoms carry a faint tint of luminous green.

At the upper end of the glen we came upon one of the finest of the gorge's wild flowers, *Trillium grandiflorum*. This is a larger, snow-white cousin of the red wake-robin, with tapered two-inch petals elegantly ruffled along the edges. Known by its more common name, large-flowered white trillium, it is one of 18 members of the lily family represented along the Mianus. Others include the tiny golden trout lily; the large spotted Canada lily; Canada mayflower, or wild lily of the valley, which carpets the forest floor; and the false hellebore, whose leaves rise from wet spots on the trail.

Like virtually all the early spring flowers we were to see on our walk, the trilliums and other woodland lilies are well adapted to life on the moist floors of deciduous woods. Drawing on the food stored over the winter in their enlarged roots and bulbs, they begin growing before their leaves unfold and start to photosynthesize. After they leaf, they bloom vigorously for a few weeks, and then begin storing food for the following season.

The deciduous woods along the upper part of the river are a mixture of red oak, black birch, beech and maple. As we entered the steeper, moister, cooler reaches of the gorge, hemlocks began to appear. The trail brought us for a moment to the river's edge, where a rock sparkled with a shiny mat of moss dotted with tiny violets. Startled by our approach, a pair of mallard ducks splashed up from the water and took off pell-mell upstream. In a tree above us we could see a flash of orange and black among the branches and hear the liquid call of a male Baltimore oriole.

Rising up from the river, the path led us along the steepening hillside and suddenly we were in the hemlock grove—a 20-acre stand of tall dark trees that Gloria Anable aptly named The Hemlock Cathedral. When we entered the grove the temperature, already chilly, seemed to

VIOLETS AND MOSS AT STREAMSIDE

drop abruptly another 10°. Through the deep forest of pillar-like trunks, random shafts of sunlight glinted upon flat sprays of hemlock needles and spotlighted verdant carpets of Canada mayflower on the springy russet forest floor.

The hemlock is a patient tree, and very particular about where it grows. Because its seedlings cannot stand direct sunlight or baking drought, they must find a place where sun-loving trees have grown up to pro-

THE HEMLOCK CATHEDRAL

vide shade. They also prefer the north- or east-facing slope of a ravine where the hottest sun seldom penetrates and where moister earth yields ample water for the hemlock's thirsty roots.

When the ground has become rich enough with generations of leaf mold from the deciduous trees, the hemlock moves in. Slowly rising above its neighbors, it gradually kills them off until its only company is the shade-tolerant beech. Eventually the hemlocks become a stable, self-perpetuating forest, like the one we were standing in. Here tiny hemlocks rose everywhere beneath their parents' sheltering boughs. We could see little else growing on the dark forest floor, save for a few flat clumps of wiry ground pine and the fronds of shade-loving lady ferns.

A Hoary Old Hemlock

At a bend in the trail we came upon the largest hemlock in the preserve, a giant that had been determined by a core sample to be over 300 years old. Its trunk, more than three feet thick, was encased by heavily furrowed bark. These trees had clearly never been cut, though entire stands of hemlock nearby were once felled for their bark, valued for a high tannin content. Indians pounded the bark of young trees into a paste that they used as poultices for sores and wounds. White settlers preferred the thicker bark of larger trees from which they extracted the tannic acid, which was used in curing leather. Acres of hemlocks were hacked down and half stripped, the trunks wastefully left on the ground to rot. Protected now, the ancient giants in this grove can probably count on a good many more years, perhaps even a century—barring a natural calamity.

LEAVES OF GROUND PINE

A GLACIER-CARRIED BOULDER

FRONDS OF LADY FERN

Toward the southern edge of the hemlock grove Bob and I stopped to admire an especially beautiful boulder molded into fluid contours by the heat and pressure of some drawn-out earth upheaval many millions of years ago. Its presence was a reminder of the forces that had made the gorge, for it had been torn out of the underlying gneiss bedrock by an ice-age glacier grinding southward. As the ice retreated, leaving the valley to be gouged deeper by a massive torrent of meltwater, it had dropped this boulder in its present position.

Near the boulder we noticed little bits of silvery material scattered through the woods, winking at us among the reddish leaves below the trail. These were pieces of local mica, the tough, heat-resistant and translucent mineral at one time widely used in lanterns, for furnace peepholes and as the windows of old-fashioned stoves. The particular variety found here, mostly embedded in the bedrock gneiss, is known as muscovite or Muscovy glass, so named because in Russia it was once used for domestic windowpanes.

Down in the ravine, off the trail, we could see other rock outcroppings that drew our curiosity. Clambering down to the river 150 feet below, we again identified the rocks as gneiss. But this time, along with the mica, we could see veins of feldspar and quartz, which intruded

MICA ON THE FOREST FLOOR

here and there through the gneiss.

These veins were a clue to another aspect of the gorge's social history, for they were the target of local mining operations until as recently as 1939. Feldspar was particularly in demand—ground up, it makes an effective household scouring powder. Along with pegmatite and quartz it was used in making pottery, enamel and glass. There was a large mine nearby at Bedford, New York, and exploratory pits were dug in the gorge. A trail of glittering mica flakes led us to one: a cavity in the hillside, where bands of rose quartz, once laid open by men with picks and shovels, were now overgrown with dripping moss.

In the Footsteps of Indians

Colonial miners were not the first to gather prized minerals from the

OUTCROPS OF GNEISS IN THE GORGE

gorge: stone arrowheads and hatchet blades have been found here and crude pieces of cooking implements have been unearthed along the banks of the stream. In fact, the river itself was named after Mayn Myanos, a chieftain of the Siwanoi tribe, which once held hunting rights to the gorge and the river lands below. In the fighting that erupted between the Indians and the Dutch and English settlers in the early 1640s, Myanos proudly put his own life on the line. Hearing that the settlers believed one good white man was more than a match for several Indians in battle, he donned his war bonnet, gathered his weapons and set out alone to give this boast the lie. Somewhere south of the gorge he encountered a Captain Patrick and two other men; engaging them without hesitation, he killed one of Patrick's companions and seriously wounded the other before the captain shot him dead. Later, in 1643, most of Myanos' remaining clansmen—some 600 people—were massacred in a punitive expedition. Despite the tribal slaughter, a few Siwanois lingered in the region until the early 1800s.

Climbing back up to rejoin the trail at the top of the gorge, we continued through the upland forest, largely a second-growth mixture of beech, birch and maple. We crossed over several stone walls, crumbling reminders of the days when the settlers had cleared their newly won land of trees and glacial boulders to make it usable for pasturage or crops. With the land abandoned and the forest taking over again, the walls now served mainly as snug

MOSS-COVERED ROSE QUARTZ

homes for chipmunks, which we glimpsed scampering over the stones on their daily rounds. The walls and the natural stone formations scattered throughout the forest are also favorite haunts for copperheads, which, along with timber rattlers, are the only poisonous snakes in the region. They often come out to bask on the rocks in the sun. Perhaps it wasn't warm enough for copperheads to show themselves this early in the season, but in any case we were to see no snakes that day —save for one small garter snake that on spotting us beat a hasty retreat into the brush.

The day became warm enough for mayflies, however; they suddenly began circling in dense, dark clouds around us, getting into our nostrils, eyes and ears. Hoping for a breeze to help brush them away, and beginning to think about lunch, we climbed a side trail through the forest. Our pathway was illuminated here and there by the gleaming white

A DILAPIDATED STONE WALL

FLOWERING DOGWOOD IN THE UPLAND FOREST

sprays of flowering dogwood as we hiked up to a 250-foot knob of bare rock called High Tor, the area's highest point.

Here we found a fine view of the hills across the gorge and of the reservoir glimmering through newly leafing trees off to the south. We ate our sandwiches under a tall, budding sassafras tree, sitting on a lichen-covered slab of rock. Around us were the slick leaves of mountain laurel and the rose-colored buds of sweet lowbush blueberries just starting to come into blossom. The sky was a rare shade of cerulean, the sandwiches were delicious, and I stretched out for a while to watch the clouds float by.

After lunch, we scrambled down the far side of High Tor and picked up the trail through the woods again. More flowers to investigate: the violet-pink blossoms of wild geraniums (which bear no relationship to the potted plant of the same name); tiny white flower clusters of early saxifrage and false Solomon's-seal; dazzling rue anemone with its clusters of lemony anthers and its distinctive three-lobed leaves. In a low place along the path a miniature bog had formed, its edges bright green with moss and its center a pea soup of algae and duckweed. On the moist margins grew one of the daintiest of all the early flowers, the tiny spring beauty, its pale pink petals delicately etched with dark pink veins. The sight of them reminded me that spring beauties are favorites of my young daughters—perhaps for their fragile look; perhaps, too, because they are so sensitive to light and temperature. On a sunny day you will find them smiling openly, but if the next day is cloudy and cool every blossom will be closed up tight.

A BUDDING BLUEBERRY BRANCH

A Floral Discovery

Just as we were about to turn down a side path to our final stopping place, Bob noticed something off in the woods: it looked like a tiny cluster of orchids, a spike of flowers scarcely eight inches high rising from a pair of smooth, veined leaves. Consulting my paperback guide to wild flowers, I triumphantly declared it to be a showy orchis, each violet, hooded flower unmistakably contrasting with a white lip and spur

RUE ANEMONE

SPRING BEAUTIES

SHOWY ORCHIS

AN EASTERN PAINTED TURTLE

A MAT OF MOSS

below. We had found one of the eight species of orchids that grow along the Mianus—and the earliest one to bloom.

Down the path and over the snaking roots of hemlocks bordering one last tributary, and we came to the end of our miniwilderness walk at Havemeyer Falls, which is named for one of the principal donors of land in the preserve. An eastern painted turtle sunning himself on a log plopped hurriedly into the water and disappeared. We had the place to ourselves.

As waterfalls go, Havemeyer is, admittedly, somewhat smaller than Niagara and Bridalveil, negotiating as it does a modest series of cascades and culminating in a drop of perhaps 15 feet. It is, however, just about the right size for a woodland waterfall of the kind that you can get to know on a personal basis. It slides, curls, tumbles and twists with just the right combination of verve and well-behaved restraint, sending perfectly symmetrical ripples across the little pool held by broken boulders at its base. Around the falls, in a scene that evokes a childhood vision of a secret retreat, a rich green rock garden flourished in the highly humid air—a jungly assortment of mosses, ferns and cresses pierced by rivulets that created their own miniature waterfall tableaux within the larger one. Bob and I must have spent a good hour just watching those sparkling little landscapes, and listening to the soft syllables of falling water, before we finally walked back up the gorge on our way home.

Everett D. Hendricks, M.D.
1955 Ruth Street
Prescott, Arizona 86301

THE LOWER POOL AT HAVEMEYER FALLS

4/ A Cosmopolitan Crew

Some people call it the Tree of Heaven. . . . It is the only tree that grows out of cement. . . . It would be considered beautiful except that there are too many of it.

BETTY SMITH/ *A TREE GROWS IN BROOKLYN*

It is a cherished—and quite accurate—dictum among New Yorkers that one has to be smart, resourceful and above all tough to survive in their high-powered town. And what goes for people goes for animals and plants as well—in some ways more so, because in such an environment man, not nature, supposedly makes the rules. Nevertheless an astonishing number of species have adjusted to urban living and even flourish, not only in New York, but in every metropolis across the land. Like the human populations of our cities, they are a distinctly cosmopolitan crew, some native to North America, a large percentage foreign born. Yet regardless of their origins they share certain faculties for survival, which in most cases include an impressive ability to take advantage of their cohabitants—us.

Some plants and animals, indeed, cope with the facts of city life with an adaptive vigor that any harassed and crowded human might envy. For example, the steady shrinkage of open green space bothers the ailanthus tree not at all; it simply shoots up through cracks in the pavement, thriving as if it had an acre of garden to itself. The problem of keeping warm on cold city nights is readily solved by starlings, which roost on electric signs; moreover, they favor those with incandescent bulbs, whose higher heat is more effective than neon in staving off the cold. The housing shortage is no problem at all for some animal species. One young woman in New York's borough of the Bronx went up to the roof of her five-story apartment house to get some sun, and came face to face with an opossum, seemingly bent on the same mission. In the city of Cincinnati, raccoons hole up in sewers, dumps, garages and places even more implausible: one raccoon was routed out of the ventilation ducts of a high-rise office building, and another, a female, was found raising her brood of four in an unused sofa on the third floor of a private house. Some of these animals have also been discovered using storm drains as regular travel routes, thus neatly avoiding the hazards of the streets above.

That familiar inhabitant of city parks, the bushy-tailed gray squirrel, has learned to be even more traffic shy than the raccoon, refusing in many cases to roam beyond the narrow bounds of the family breeding ground. One interesting evolutionary result is that squirrel concentrations only a few blocks apart may vary considerably in color, one group becoming albinistic, or off-white, and the other melanistic, or black. Those few squirrels that dare the streets do so with a sophisticated care that would warm the heart of any human mother. One dedicated squirrel watcher in Manhattan's Stuyvesant Square Park, which is bisected by a broad avenue open to passing cars, swears that the squirrels there have learned to wait for the traffic light to flash the "walk" signal, and then to cross only in the white-lined path marked for pedestrians. So far as my informant can recall, there has been only one automotive incident, involving a male squirrel that had spotted a female of the species across the avenue and was apparently on a reckless errand of love. He paid for his disregard of the traffic code as might any jaywalker, with his life.

However, the urban squirrel with enough sense to stay off the streets has a better life expectancy than does its country cousin. For such traditional enemies as hawks and weasels no longer frequent the heart of the city, and the squirrels themselves are busy breeders—some produce two litters of four young per year. A gift for proliferating is, in fact, a major key to the success of any species, animal or plant, in coping with the pitfalls of the urban environment. Though many a seed will never take root, nor many a hatchling last through the first year of life, quantity reproduction ensures that enough will survive to keep the species alive.

A second indispensable key to urban survival is the ability of certain animals to scavenge, to capitalize on anything that is left over in human habitats—scraps of food, leftover space for use as nesting, denning or growing sites, even the unused time of night when human beings are asleep and when foraging invites less danger from dogs, cars and small boys with BB guns.

Beyond question, the most accomplished scavenger of them all is the herring gull, more commonly, if mistakenly, called the sea gull. Like the gray squirrel, the gull is a native American of long lineage. By the time the *Mayflower* hove into sight off Plymouth Rock in 1620, this handsome gray-and-white bird had acquired the habit of greeting incoming ships, soaring patiently astern with bright eyes to spot garbage being tossed over the rail. Today it regularly patrols not only coastal ports like New York, Boston, San Francisco and Los Angeles, but also Chicago, St. Louis and other lake and river cities. So wide a range is possible because the gull is not strictly a bird of the open sea, as its popular name would suggest, but is equally at home far inland, wherever land and water meet. In these so-called edge environments it finds food, drink and resting places on both water and dry ground. A superb flying machine, it can also swim and move around on land more adeptly than most birds.

A rare melanistic squirrel, a member of the gray species born with black hair due to inbreeding of a recessive gene, scurries along a wooden erosion fence at Manhattan's Inwood Hill. Its distinctive color would make it easy prey under completely wild conditions, but the security of Inwood—and a few other parks where the black squirrel occurs—has aided its survival.

Though the gull prefers to drink fresh water, it can thrive just as well on salt water, straining out excess salt through glands above its eyes and ejecting it through openings in its bill. Solid fare presents no problem at all. Along with the vulture, the gull is probably the champion omnivore among birds, possessing a cast-iron stomach and corrosive digestive juices that allow it to consume almost anything, grinding up its food internally with the efficiency of a kitchen-sink garbage disposer. Aided by its excellent eyesight, it can locate anything remotely edible almost a mile off: all varieties of fish—alive or dead, in bits, washed ashore or thrown overboard from boats; scraps of hot dogs, buns and other burnt offerings from public piers and beaches; and assorted other refuse that makes sewer outlets, garbage scows and city dumps the species' favorite hunting grounds.

To appease its appetite, the gull has even adapted some old tricks to new and risky surroundings. Drivers on busy highways around New York and other cities occasionally report seeing a gull soar in over the pavement ahead of them, drop a scallop, clam or mussel on the hard surface, then swoop down to snatch away the fractured prize a split second ahead of the onrushing cars. Players on municipal links have also been astonished to see gulls zero in on their golf balls and make off with them, perhaps mistaking them for duck eggs.

When I watch thousands of gulls wheeling and screaming over the incoming garbage trucks on the marshy margins of New York's Staten Island or Jamaica Bay, I find it hard to believe that less than a century ago these relentless scavengers had almost disappeared from the North Atlantic coast. Gulls have always nested in large colonies on shorelines and offshore islands. In a completely wild environment, the birds have proved big and tough enough to discourage other animals from raiding their ground-level nests by flying at them, hitting them with their beaks and flailing at them with their wings. But they could not stop determined market hunters from scooping up barrelfuls of eggs or killing thousands of adult birds for the white breast feathers and black-tipped wing feathers highly valued by the 19th Century millinery trade. Today, with the slaughter long since banned by federal law, and with little natural competition and a limitless larder, herring gulls may be more numerous than ever; one estimate of their numbers in the New York area runs as high as a million.

Some ornithologists fear that such concentrations may drive out smaller wild species like the tern, which has already disappeared from some of its former nesting sites as a result of competition from the territorially fiercer gull. Still, even the gull's critics admit the bird is a useful sanitarian, cleaning up carrion and other reeking refuse. And nature-loving city dwellers are happy to have the gull around, soaring on its long, tapered wings with casual grace, the sound of its mewing cry an evocation of sky and sea.

Many of the same people would gladly dispense with two other bird species that crowd the urban scene: the starling and the common street pigeon. The root of the trouble, in the case of both birds, is their extreme gregariousness and noisiness, the latter being especially true of the starling. They tend to gang up in such numbers, whether feeding or just roosting, that the din—not to mention the stench—can be overpowering. In the nation's capital, preparations for every recent Presidential inauguration have included spraying the trees along Pennsylvania Avenue with a starling-repellent chemical so that parade watchers could stand beneath them with confidence. The cost to the taxpayer of this policy comes to about $10,000 per spraying session.

On less august occasions, whenever and wherever harried citizens have decided that the birds have become an unbearable public nuisance, various other measures to disperse the flocks have been employed, usually to little avail. Some of the antibird forces try to stun the noisy starlings into silence, and drive them off in fright, with even louder noisemakers—clashing cymbals, rolling drums, booming cannons and the recorded screams of their fearsome natural enemy, the eagle. In one Pennsylvania college town, two professors seized a starling, held it upside down, recorded its anguished squawks, then played the distress call at various starling roosts. The strategy failed dismally at roosts that happened also to be occupied by house sparrows and grackles. The starlings did, indeed, flee; but then they looked back, saw their fellow tenants still placidly in possession, and promptly rejoined them.

Specialized tactics have been tried against pigeons, too, including the deployment of plastic replicas of two of their ancient foes—the snake and the owl—on building ledges, sills and other sites in the city where the birds like to congregate. The pigeon's pursuers have also called in science, aiming not at mere dispersal but at actually curbing the pigeon population explosion by means of a chemical sterilant mixed into bait food. But the stuff is expensive; furthermore, it would have to be spread far and wide—and fast—to keep up with the pigeon birth rate: some of the female birds produce as many as 11 broods, two babies in each brood, every 12 months.

However, I don't want to leave the impression that pigeons and starlings are nothing but bad news for the city dweller. Their histories alone hold a certain fascination. Ironically enough, the starling, a native of the European continent, was imported as a cultural asset. This move was the inspiration of a 19th Century man-about-New York named Eugene Schieffelin. Besides being a bird lover, Schieffelin was a Shakespeare enthusiast who decided that his fellow citizens would be elevated by knowing at firsthand all the birds mentioned by the Bard in his plays. Schieffelin had tried to introduce nightingales, skylarks and chaffinches to the city, but none had survived. In 1890 he purchased 60 starlings—acclaimed for their abilities as mimics in Shakespeare's *Henry IV*—and let them go in Central Park.

Schieffelin repeated the gesture the next year with 40 more, and at that point the starlings' own zest for multiplying took over. The spread of this seed flock, at first slow, became so explosive that by 1950 starlings were part- or full-time residents of all the 48 contiguous United States, every Canadian province, and a good deal of Northern Mexico as well. Federal survey figures tabulated in the early 1970s show the starling increasing at a faster rate than any other North American bird, native or immigrant.

The pigeon's history in America predates the starling's by more than a century; in fact, the pigeon's habit of living with people and their

Of all the creatures that have adjusted to urban life, these six birds—along with the herring gull—are among the most successful. Snugged down in the myriad niches of New York, house sparrows, pigeons and starlings have proliferated into the millions. Less numerous but just as secure are the Chinese ring-necked pheasant, found along parkway margins; the mute swan, which floats serenely on ponds; and the cattle egret, an immigrant to Jamaica Bay from Florida pastures.

CHINESE RING-NECKED PHEASANT

CATTLE EGRET

HOUSE SPARROW

PIGEON

MUTE SWAN

STARLING

crotchets goes back at least 6,500 years. Also known as the rock dove, *Columba livia,* it first left its natural nesting sites on the cliffs of the Middle Eastern foothills about 4500 B.C. to live in the temples and houses of the earliest Mesopotamian civilizations. It was subsequently domesticated for eating by the ancient Egyptians, Greeks and Romans, and was later raised for the same purpose in dovecotes all over Europe. Brought to America by early colonists along with pigs, apple trees, herbs, flowers and other cargo useful for getting a start in the New World, the rock dove continued to find its way to the dinner table, especially in its tender young form as squab. It was also bred as a pet, for racing and—alias the homing pigeon—for messenger duty.

With the advent of the domesticated chicken, the telegraph and the telephone, pigeons declined in popularity as food and friend of man—but zoomed in numbers. No longer penned or provided with dovecotes, they were left on their own, mostly around the growing cities, and proceeded to demonstrate their ancient knack for adjusting to the unpredictable ways of their human neighbors—for example, the modern penchant for building boxlike skyscrapers that provide no footholds for birds. Undaunted, the pigeons continue to seek out ornate older buildings, bridge girders and other high, safe roosting places that are quite adequate substitutes for the rocky cliffs used by the ancestral breed. And when they swoop down to cadge a handout from kindly pedestrians, some instinct—perhaps based on their traditional role in the human diet—makes them stay just out of reach, though in Manhattan's poorest neighborhoods an occasional pigeon does find its way to table as "Central Park pheasant."

For many New Yorkers with neither the means nor the time to get out into the country, an afternoon spent feeding bread crumbs to pigeons in the park is a chance to make direct contact with one of the most venerable species of wildlife still extant. For this reason alone the pigeon has earned its keep in the city. The starling, for its part, is perhaps even more deserving; it digs up millions of cutworms and other insect grubs before they can assault vegetation. And, as Shakespeare claimed, it is indeed an entertaining mimic: it imitates the calls of at least 50 other birds such as towhees, catbirds and jays so skillfully that experts often cannot tell the difference. I have heard starlings mimic robins well enough to fool me until I actually saw the source of the sound, and I am told they can also do fairly good takeoffs on cats, dogs, and—of particular comfort to city folk—police whistles.

Of all the alien species that have made themselves at home in American cities, one seems to have been visited upon us solely in retribution for our sins. The brown, or sewer, rat, unlike the pigeon and the starling, arrived uninvited and has been unwelcome ever since. More formally known as *Rattus norvegicus,* or Norway rat (because it was first scientifically described in that country), it is believed to have landed on these shores as a shipboard stowaway around 1775. The brown rat enjoys the same special advantage as the pigeon in its adaptability to modern city life: it has lived in close proximity to people for thousands of years, thriving on pilfered grain and scavenged slops. It carried this handy habit from Asia, its presumed place of origin, to Europe, migrating both overland and by ship, and eventually across the Atlantic.

In urban America the brown rat's favorite habitat is a slum neighborhood, though occasionally it surfaces on such thoroughfares as New York's Park Avenue, causing the swank tenantry to brood about civilization's onrushing end. Usually, however, the ghetto's dilapidated buildings provide the brown rat with a superior choice of nesting holes and runs. There it lives in packs and defends its turf against intruding rats, including its coimmigrant, *Rattus rattus,* the black, or roof, rat. The more easily accessible garbage in the slum areas provides ample fare, and by feeding during the night the rat generally manages to avoid contact with vengeful humans.

As for its natural predators, such as foxes and snakes, most of them have been obligingly banished beyond the city limits. And taking into account the rat's high reproductive rate—a healthy female can produce up to 12 litters a year, with as many as 10 offspring in each—some estimates place the rat population in the United States at one per human inhabitant. This grim statistic, however, should be taken with a large dose of skepticism. Some years ago a research team financed by Rockefeller funds made a count of New York's rat populace and came up with a figure of 250,000—and considerable doubt even about that. One researcher conceded he had no way of knowing how many times, in the course of descending from floor to floor of a building, he had counted the same rat descending with him.

Though there are not many city dwellers willing to say a good word for *Rattus norvegicus,* a few rat lovers actually do exist—including, quite possibly, the members of a sewer maintenance crew who were repairing some underground damage in Manhattan one day in 1974. As they worked, a passel of rats looked on; then, suddenly, the animals turned and fled. The men took this as a sign of danger and scrambled up to the street, just in time to avoid being overcome by gas fumes the rats had already detected.

In a less-accidental way, rats are becoming benefactors of man. Through long centuries of sharing his food, housing and environment, they have become immensely useful reflectors of human behavior. Laboratories, of course, test specially bred white rats; but more recently brown rats have been studied, and in their own quarters. Observers have found that the healthiest and smartest animals are those that were raised in the "best" sections of a rat community; those subjected to crowded conditions and inadequate fare soon display criminal tendencies—stealing, fighting one another and even in some cases resorting to cannibalism. "With what we have learned from the rats," says New York zoologist E. M. Reilly Jr., "we may be able to look to our own selves, hopefully, with more success."

Two red-fox pups venture warily from their underground den. Though still hunted for sport, for their fur and as vermin, members of this species have actually expanded their range with the spread of the suburbs; they not only prefer cleared woodland to deep forest, but they find food in backyard duck ponds and rabbit hutches.

For other mammals, urban crowding has meant a scramble for the fringes of woods and the thickets of brush that still hold out against the advance of paving, serving as protective cover by day and a base from which to forage by night. Cemeteries, often the largest tracts of green land left within city limits, are especially notable for affording both. In these lavishly landscaped anterooms to the afterworld, the trees are generally old and large, providing a plentiful supply of nesting places and nuts; smaller, ornamental plantings offer a diversified menu of berries and fruits. Human visitors, moreover, are allowed in only during stated hours, and then are expected to maintain respectful control over their cars, children and dogs; from late afternoon until eight or nine the next morning the local wildlife has these places pretty much to itself. In one sizable cemetery several red foxes were seen stealthily patrolling among the crypts and gravestones. The reasons for the foxes' presence was soon evident; a researcher who made a painstaking count of the squirrels in the cemetery found 4,000—as high a ratio per acre as in many rural areas. The foxes were nature's way of trying to hold the squirrel population in check—although they did vary their menu with an occasional chipmunk.

Unless an animal watcher is exceptionally vigilant, however, the shrewd red fox is more often sensed than seen. In the upper reaches of the Bronx, a number of citizens use the tiny plots behind their row houses to grow grapes and vegetables, and even to raise chickens. Sometimes, overnight, one of the fowl disappears; the speed and silence of the snatch point to only one predator—a fox.

Everett D. Hendricks, M.D.
[illegible] Ruth Street
Prescott, Arizona 86301

It is in suburban surroundings that the wildlife of a metropolitan area is most visible and most at ease. Not that all hazards of urban living can be escaped in suburbia; witness the number of skunk, raccoon and opossum casualties on former country roads that have graduated into turnpikes. Still, suburbs provide more of the living and roaming space and food sources needed by animals—especially larger ones like deer. I can count a good dozen times when, driving home to Connecticut after a day in Manhattan, I spotted the bright rump of a white-tailed deer bounding through a patch of woods along the road.

In the land around my house, animals come and go often enough for me to have learned something of their habits and even their personalities. One of them is the raccoon. Among suburbanites, this nocturnal masked bandit's knack for getting into tightly closed garbage pails is legendary. But its ingenuity does not stop there, as a friend of mine who lives not far from me can testify.

A couple of years ago my friend found a male baby raccoon in a thicket near the house and decided to raise him as a playmate for the children (a practice not generally recommended, for some raccoons begin to bite unexpectedly as they mature, and are subject to distemper and other diseases). Zip, as the pet was named, was a generally welcome addition to the family—roughhousing, investigating every new object with comical curiosity, even playing with the kitten. But as he grew he developed a strange habit. In the dead of night he would somehow manage to get out of his pen and go over to a neighbor's house, where he would invade the kitchen through a small swinging door installed for the family cat. He would then proceed to open the icebox, take out a carton of milk or preferably a jar of maple syrup, find a box of Wheaties in the cupboard, pour out the flakes in a mound on the kitchen floor, drench them with milk or syrup and eat a hearty, early morning breakfast before going home to bed.

I admit I was skeptical enough about this story to dig into some scientific literature on the raccoon—with persuasive results. The creature, it turns out, has forepaws very much like human hands. Each paw has five digits, or fingers; each digit has three small bones, making it flexible. The forepaws are extremely sensitive—perhaps the most sensitive tactile organ of any mammal—and can be used with remarkable dexterity. A zoologist to whom I cited these facts confirmed them, but he insisted that Zip's exploit in the neighbor's kitchen had to have been a one-time accident.

This theory did not hold up, however. According to Zip's owner, his neighbor apprehended the raccoon more than once at the caper, and complained until Zip was exiled to a nearby nature preserve. That should have ended the matter, but a few days later my friend's telephone rang. This time the neighbor had found not one but two raccoons in his kitchen, neither of which he had seen before. Zip, before being returned to the wild, had apparently led some accomplices to the scene. Somehow, they had learned exactly how to pull off the Wheaties job.

I have given up trying to catch raccoons in the act myself. After more than one early morning spent picking up garbage strewn around the yard, I began to keep the garbage cans just outside the kitchen door, not only securely covered but placed inside a large, heavy-lidded wooden box. It was in the wake of this stratagem that I became acquainted, though not of my own free will, with another suburban denizen of determined bent.

I got to know the creature last December, after the garbage man announced that we had come to a parting of the ways: he said he was tired of lugging the cans out of the raccoon-proof box and up the hilly path to his truck. This turned out to be only a polite alibi; actually, he had found a skunk in the box, apparently wintering there. How it had managed to slip inside still puzzles me; in any case, though I had to lug the garbage cans myself, I left the skunk in occupancy. After all, a skunk has to sleep somewhere, and I was not about to risk a confrontation trying to kick it out. By spring, fortunately, I had signed up another garbage man, and my white-striped tenant had left.

Wherever the skunk has gone, I suspect it is doing well. Like raccoons, skunks survive not only by denning up wherever the opportunity presents itself, but also by operating when the rest of us are asleep. The skunk will eat just about anything that comes to hand, though it prefers rodents and insects. It is, in fact, one of the few animals that can clean out a yellow jacket's nest with no ill effects, thanks to a skin so thick it is stingproof.

The skunk's most notorious skill is, contrary to belief, not used capriciously. The foul sulfurous spray it emits—sometimes four or six sprays in rapid order, discharged through twin rear nozzles and accurately aimed at a distance of up to 15 feet—is a weapon the animal employs only in self-defense when it senses ultimate danger. Otherwise, the skunk is eminently peace loving.

The least contentious of suburban mammals, I think, must be the opossum. Faced with a threat, it will bare a fine set of teeth, snarl and hiss; but if this fails and it cannot flee, it will totally confound its foe

A young opossum snuggles up to its mother inside a tree stump in suburban New Jersey. Once native only to the South, the species now roams metropolitan areas throughout the Northeast. Part of the migration —according to one Long Islander—was seaborne. Ships bringing lumber from Georgia carried caged opossums on deck to slaughter for fresh meat. Some of the cages were washed up on Long Island beaches; the surviving animals broke out and made their way inland.

by feigning death—the unique survival trick known as playing 'possum. The animal suddenly goes limp; it will not move even if prodded or picked up. Scientists who have observed this phenomenon do not know whether it is a deliberate tactic or a state of catatonic shock, but they do know that the opossum's heart rate slows down, and that it can play dead for as long as six hours.

Away from its enemies, the opossum seems to spend much of its time propagating the species—two litters a year, each with as many as 18 offspring. Like infant kangaroos and wallabies in Australia but no other American animal, the female opossum has a nursing pouch into which her offspring—less than an inch long at birth—crawl and stay for three months before facing life outside.

Nor is the opossum's status as our only native marsupial its sole distinction: it is also our oldest native mammal. Skeleton fossils of its ancestors, dug out of Wyoming rock formations dating back a million years, can hardly be differentiated from a modern opossum skeleton. It is unlikely that even the spreading hazards of suburbia will snuff the species out.

For plants, the problems of urban and suburban living are little different from those that plague the animal and human inhabitants: soot, the spewings of automobile exhausts and the noxious wastes of spreading industrial enterprise are all hazardous to their health. In addition, a separate peril for vegetation lurks in the nature of the soil, particularly in the city proper; it tends to be overly dry and compacted—a condition hardly conducive to riotous growth.

Yet many plants defy the odds against them in the urban environment; they do more than survive—they flourish. No better proof of this exists than in so-called disturbance communities. This very apt term is a relatively recent one and says a good deal about the changing face of the American landscape. A disturbance community is a plant community that has developed on a site where the original environment has been transformed to meet the needs of an expanding human population. Such sites include city lots that have been cleared, the sides of turnpikes and highway cloverleafs, railroad rights of way, and areas dug up for the installation of telephone and power transmission lines.

I have tramped a number of these places in and around New York. One of the most interesting is a railroad track, now largely unused, that bisects Van Cortlandt Park in the Bronx and at several points opens on small swampy patches threaded by Tibbetts Brook. On a day in late

June, I counted 50 different plant species—and they were only the ones I could identify. A lovely collection they were: hedge bindweed, a wild morning-glory with white trumpet-shaped flowers twining up a rusty chain link fence; common mullein, its light green leaves ascending a tall, clublike stalk topped by yellow blossoms; musk mallow, its pink-lavender petals like those of a wild rose; the reddish-purple spikes of viper's bugloss; the yellow-and-orange pouches of toadflax, more commonly called butter-and-eggs.

In summer, New York and other urban areas bloom with the bright colors of weeds in flower. The hardy plants shown here, whose ancestral seeds were accidentally imported to America, take root wherever land is cleared—in fields and city dumps, at the sides of highways, and even in sidewalk cracks.

At the edge of one swampy patch, two especially tall and graceful plants vied for attention and living space. One was purple loosestrife, growing up to seven feet high, with long, upright spikes of magenta flowers. Its even taller companion—towering as high as 15 feet—was the phragmites, or common, reed with supple, rustling leaves and feathery plumes; its smaller stalks are favorites in dried-flower arrangements. As I stood for a moment admiring the plants, it occurred to me that I was seeing the same kind of phenomenon that urban humanity has come to accept as a way of life: the crowded but essentially peaceful coexistence of native and foreign born. In the case of these plants, in fact, the origins were not even discernible. Though the bamboo-like phragmites has a decidedly Oriental look, it is indigenous. The purple loosestrife, which has made itself every bit as much at home, actually came from Europe; its seeds were entangled in wool waste imported a century ago by a factory in Newburgh, a Hudson River town 60 miles north of New York City.

But in plants, as in people, coexistence is no bar to the competitive spirit. Purple loosestrife has spread so vigorously around swamps, ponds and ditches that some biologists fear it may crowd out cattails and other native aquatic plants valued as wildlife food. The phragmites proliferates with equal ease: each reed is supported by a network of underground rhizomes, or rootstalks, which store nutrients for an early start in spring and which keep the plant green and growing six months out of the year. The creeping rhizomes can extend a stand of reeds by as much as 30 feet in a year.

A rather different modus vivendi between native and foreign born prevails among wild flowers. The tender native woodland species, which produce comparatively few seeds and do not spread freely, have tended to thin out in disturbance areas. Adapted to bloom in the early spring sun before the trees come fully into leaf, they need the subsequent shade and rich woodland soil. In contrast, most of the successful

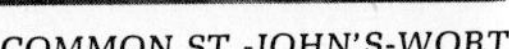

COMMON ST.-JOHN'S-WORT

QUEEN ANNE'S LACE

ASIATIC DAYFLOWER

DEPTFORD PINK

PURPLE LOOSESTRIFE

NIGHTSHADE

DANDELION

Sturdy American elms, once a familiar sight in United States towns and cities, shade a broad avenue off New York's Central Park just before World War I. In the decades following 1930, a blight devastated the species. A European strain of elm planted to replace the dead trees was subsequently found to be resistant to the disease, and today about 95 per cent of Central Park's elms are the hardier, foreign-born variety.

immigrants are tough and vigorous. They can grow in poor soil and take lots of sun; generally they have hairy leaves and stems to conserve moisture in hot, open sites, whether in the city itself or in outlying areas.

A good many of the most tenacious, abundant and colorful flowers of wayside and field, in fact, are aliens: Queen Anne's lace—the wild carrot—whose flat-topped clusters of tiny white blooms toss along busy highways in summertime like spume in the wake of a ship; bouncing Bet, a blowzy Cockney beauty with cheeky petals of pale pink or white; the field, or common, daisy, the orange day lily, and such other familiars as red clover, white clover, peppermint, spearmint, mustard and forget-me-nots. Leaving their lands of origin has not harmed these species at all. They are in flower during most of the summer, produce prodigious amounts of seeds (the common daisy can produce more than a thousand seeds on a single plant) and spread with utter abandon. That, of course, is the reason why naturalists plead with Sunday walkers not to pick the woodland orchids and trilliums, but you may help yourself to Queen Anne's lace.

Grasses and weeds provide further proof of alien triumphs. The grass fondly known as Kentucky bluegrass is actually Eurasian; the most notorious weeds that invade suburban lawns—crab grass and dandelion—are European. As one who must regularly ply a lawn mower, I have mixed feelings about these species. But there is one alien weed whose persistence I cannot help admiring, if only because of its long and fascinating connection with the history of our country. The broad-leafed plantain, whose leaf vaguely resembles a shoe sole, followed the early settlers west so doggedly that the Indians called it white man's footstep. I put this down to sheer imagery until I learned that plantain seeds literally can cross country by foot. A mucilaginous substance they contain makes them gluey when wet; they stick to the soles of shoes and travel right along.

But of all immigrant plant species, trees have scored some of the most notable successes in adapting to urban life. It is a curious fact that the majority of the trees that now prosper in cities originated in very different surroundings in Asia or Europe. Among those favored for street and park planting, the names are indicative: London plane, Norway maple, European linden, Russian olive, Japanese cherry. Though not so explicitly labeled, one of the finest trees in California parks and suburbs, the eucalyptus, is a subtropical species introduced from Australia by professional plant hunters and clipper-ship captains in the middle of the 19th Century.

They also brought back the ginkgo, or maidenhair, tree, now popular for sidewalk planting in Manhattan and elsewhere because it is easily propagated, grows slowly and is not affected in the slightest by insects, diseases, smoke, gases or compacted soil. A "living fossil," as Darwin called it, the ginkgo is at least 100 million years old and in fact once was native to North America; it survived the ice ages only in parts of the Orient, however, where it was sheltered as a temple tree. Apparently the ginkgo has lived so long, and gone through so many adversities, that its less adaptable strains have disappeared, leaving a tree that is tolerant even of the stresses of modern city life.

Certain native trees, too, such as the locust and the pin oak, seem able to withstand the punishments of the urban environment, but two of the most beloved and widespread of the American species have virtually disappeared. A few generations ago the chestnut and the elm provided both shade and majestic beauty in residential neighborhoods; today they are rarities, struggling against total extinction.

It was not the competition of foreign trees but another sort of alien invasion that defeated the chestnut and the elm. In the 1890s a deadly fungus—now known as chestnut blight—came in on shipments of young Chinese chestnut trees; it spread to wipe out the prized native species throughout its range in the East. Around 1930 another notorious fungus, Dutch elm disease, arrived by way of the logs of European elms imported for manufacture into the fancy, swirl-grained furniture that was then the mode. Carried from tree to tree by the elm bark beetle, the disease is still costing us many of our finest elms every year.

Recently a fungicide that had been used for peanut crops attacked by a blight similar to elm disease has been experimentally injected into the soil surrounding the elms, and it shows some promise of bringing relief: of 300 elms so treated on Long Island in 1973, all but 10 were still flourishing two years later. The outlook for the chestnut is not yet clear. The trees that do survive seldom exceed a height of 15 feet—they once rose as tall as 100 feet—and though they may live long enough to bear nuts, they rarely last for more than 20 years. There is some talk among dendrologists of producing a hybrid, a cross between the native species and the Chinese chestnut, which seems slightly less vulnerable to disease. Purists who yearn for the native's return have their own pet idea: they have launched a campaign to collect the nuts of apparently healthy, young American chestnuts, hoping to propagate those that seem disease resistant and most likely to produce healthy offspring.

Not long ago I had a poignant insight into the chestnut's plight. I was walking with a friend through the woods behind his suburban house when suddenly he stopped and pointed to a mere sprig of a tree, whiplike, no more than about three feet tall, bearing a few small leaves.

"Know what this is?" my friend asked. I shook my head.

"An American chestnut, believe it or not," he said. "Every year it grows to about this height, maybe a foot or so more, then the fungus hits it and it dies. But then, the next year, it's up again. The roots keep it alive, and it makes another try."

We walked on in silence. "I guess," my friend said after a while, "it's waiting for a cure for the blight."

I think about that little tree from time to time, and I wish it well.

A Chinese ginkgo tree in Manhattan, a species imported 200 years ago, spreads a bright autumnal umbrella that rises more than 100 feet.

How real the hope is for the comeback of the species no one can say. Perhaps its very tenacity will save it; that is not a trait to be underestimated in trees.

There is a kind of model for the chestnut in a very different species, once alien to these shores, which more than any other tree seems to sum up the virtues of tenacity in a tough environment. It is an Asian import, the ailanthus, celebrated in Betty Smith's popular novel of tenement life in early 20th Century New York, *A Tree Grows in Brooklyn.*

In point of fact, the ailanthus grows in all the other four New York City boroughs as well; it may also be found from the slums of Newark to the affluent suburbs of Westchester County and clear on across the United States. More properly the tree is called *Ailanthus altissima;* "ailanthus" is a botanical Latinization of the Indonesian *ailanto,* meaning tree of heaven. Some people who consider the ailanthus less than heavenly call it stinkweed, after the admittedly foul odor of its crushed leaves and of the flowers borne by the male trees.

By whatever name, the tree makes its appearance everywhere, wanted or not, sticking up out of backyards, alleyways, broken sidewalks, vacant lots. It has soft and brittle wood that is useless for lumber, and its roots, like those of the willow, have an annoying habit of breaking or clogging pipes and drains as they search for water.

The tree can, and frequently does, shoot skyward at a rate of eight feet a year. Moreover, even if it is cut down one year, the next year several young trees are likely to sprout from the stump, forming an incipient thicket that seems to defy cutting again. Like a few other fierce botanical competitors, the ailanthus produces a chemical inhibitor to prevent rival species from thriving nearby. This weapon, a toxic substance given off by the tree's leaves, is rain washed to earth, where it discourages the growth of other plants. The ailanthus even has its own special traveling companion, which it brought along to this country: the large saturniid cynthia moth, a parasite whose larvae feed on the tree's grime-covered leaves in cities—though without doing any lasting harm. Curiously, the moths cannot seem to follow the tree to the countryside; as one entomologist observed in baffled wonderment, perhaps they actually *like* soot.

There is another thing about the ailanthus: it is beautiful. And perhaps even more to the point, it is there, where other trees are not. With its lacy parasols of sword-shaped leaves poking up over a backyard fence, it softens the hard lines of brownstone, brick and concrete, filtering the hot August sun into palm-frond patterns, hinting of places

Everett D. Hendricks, M.D.
1?75 Ruth Street
Prescott, Arizona 86301

people would rather be than on the city's baking streets. It was this exotic mien that impelled wealthy men to buy the tree as an ornament when it was first introduced from Asia by way of England back in 1784.

By the mid-19th Century many a discriminating American homeowner insisted on having an ailanthus planted in a prominent spot in his garden. It was especially admired for its fantastic tropical clusters of bright reddish-yellow fruits, each fruit a papery samara—twisted like an airplane propeller to be borne away on the wind. And so, as the city pushed back the forest, the tree of heaven took its place in the sun, changing from a rich man's bauble into a poor man's solace. It blooms in late June, bears fruit in late summer, and in fall its leaves turn a delicate orange. Though in the fresh air of the country it may attain the age of 100 or more, in the city it lives fast and dies young, seldom surviving beyond 25 to 30 years. But its kind goes on, and on.

At the end of *A Tree Grows in Brooklyn,* the heroine, Francie Nolan, takes a last look at her backyard. The tree whose umbrellas of leaves had curled around her fire escape had been cut down by the landlord because some neighboring housewives complained that the branches got tangled in the wash drying on their lines. But lo and behold, Francie saw that a new tree had grown from the stump. It had grown out along the ground to an unshaded place with no clotheslines above it, and then had started to reach toward the sky again.

Francie pondered this miracle: "The fir tree that the Nolans had cherished with waterings and manurings had long since sickened and died. But this tree in the yard—this tree that men chopped down . . . this tree that they built a bonfire around, trying to burn up its stump—this tree lived! It lived! And nothing could destroy it."

A Wild World in Miniature

PHOTOGRAPHS BY HENRY GROSKINSKY

Hidden in the parks, streets, vacant lots, window boxes and woodland remnants of New York City and its suburbs is a wild world in miniature, an animal kingdom as thriving as that of any tropical jungle. Teeming with ferocious predators, placid herbivores, fliers, hoppers and creepers, this world is the intriguing microcosm of insects.

Insects adjust to the city more easily than do most larger wild creatures, managing to find snug homes in flower stems and in the cracks of stone walls, and moist nurseries for their young in ponds and puddles. Food is abundant—not only city vegetation but also brushes, wine-bottle corks and books. Some insects have even been found munching on museum mummies.

These ubiquitous denizens of the city present an enormous diversity of shape, size and color. Long and thin, short and round, winged and tubelike, they range from the microscopic .011 inch of a tiny parasitic wasp called the Trichogramma, to the four inches of the Chinese mantis. Their colors include virtually every shade in the spectrum: from the black and orange of the monarch butterfly to the copper-tinted blues and greens of the dogbane beetle.

The growth cycle of the insect is one of the most complex in the animal world. Though some, like the grasshopper nymph at right, emerge from the egg as miniature versions of the adult, most insects undergo a remarkable metamorphosis from the infant larva through the adolescent pupa to the sexually mature adult *(pages 116-121)*.

Once mature, insects are astonishingly prolific: the queen honeybee, for one, lays about 600,000 eggs during her lifetime. Her progeny—and those of other insects—might well overrun their urban environment were it not for two critical facts: insects are susceptible to a wide range of diseases and over half the species are carnivorous. The hunters prey on the herbivores—as well as each other—with unbridled appetites. Both hunters and hunted are also preyed upon by larger creatures—principally birds, frogs and fish. To defend themselves they have a battery of ingenious weapons and protective devices. These defenses, together with the insects' energy and extraordinary reproductive powers, keep them flourishing in a hostile world —to which they contribute the constant and fascinating whirl of motion and color.

A grasshopper in its nymph stage —smaller than the mature insect but otherwise nearly identical to it— clings to a reed near the edge of a suburban salt-water marsh. The nymph has developed a greenish hue from its diet of moist foliage; in drier areas it would turn brown. The insect's color thus helps it escape detection.

The Growth of an Insect

Few insect mothers make such elaborate preparations for their young as does the potter wasp, which builds a secure mud nest and stocks it with food for her egg—the initial life stage of all insects. Most insects simply lay their eggs on leaves or in holes they have bored in stems or in the ground, and provide no larder.

From the egg, insects develop in two ways: some, called nymphs, are small-scale, flightless versions of their elders. However, the majority of hatchlings come out as larvae, showing no resemblance in form or behavior to the adult—the larval caterpillar, for example, becomes the adult butterfly. The larva spends most of its time eating, storing food in its body for the next phase of metamorphosis, called the pupa.

Pupae are generally concealed in cocoons or hidden underground. In this stage the insect lives off stored nourishment and appears inactive, but is changing dramatically: on most species wings appear. By now, too, the insect's adult cuticle, or exoskeleton, has formed—a tough, armor-like shield that prevents body moisture from evaporating.

In the final—and often extremely short-lived—stage of metamorphosis, the adult insect becomes capable of flight and reproduction.

A female potter wasp shapes a juglike nest made of dirt mixed with saliva. When the nest is complete, she lays one egg, suspending it from the ceiling by a fine thread that she secretes.

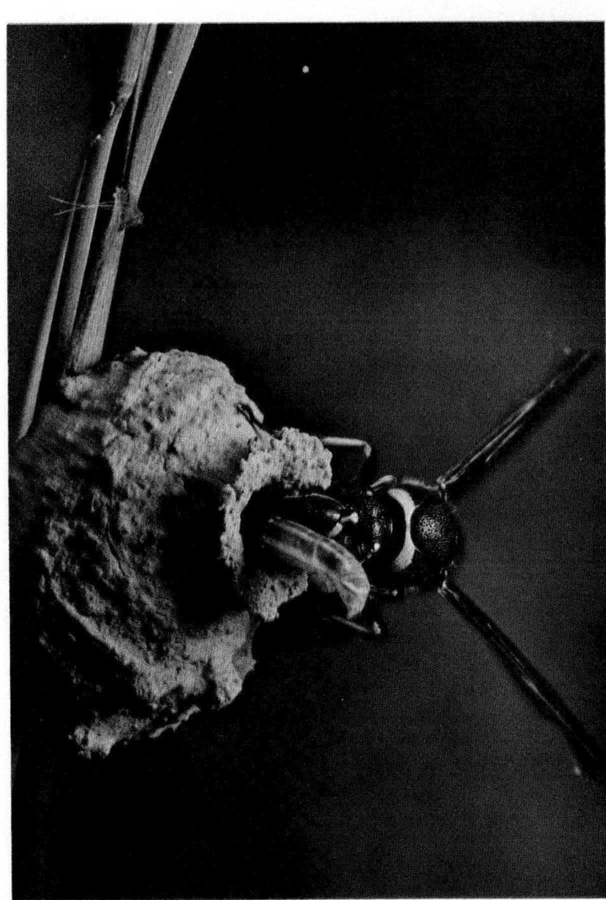

Having laid her single egg, the mother wasp pushes a caterpillar into her newly built nest. This wasp stuffed in eight caterpillars, then sealed off the entrance. When the larva hatches it feeds on the caterpillars, pupates and eventually chews through the mud wall to freedom as an adult wasp.

At left, an aphid-lion emerges from a shell deposited by its mother atop a silky filament that she secreted and attached to a leaf. Within half an hour after leaving the shell, the hatchling will descend the thread to seek its first meal, usually an aphid. If it is unsuccessful, it may crawl up a neighboring filament and devour one of its unhatched siblings.

Shown at right are two stages in a stinkbug's life. At lower center are small eggs, whose spiky crowns admit sperm for fertilization and oxygen for sustenance. Next to them are hatched nymphs with tough, dark skins. Lying upon the cluster a nymph has just molted; its new skin has not had time to harden and darken. The vivid cuticle colors warn predators that the insect secretes a malodorous repellent.

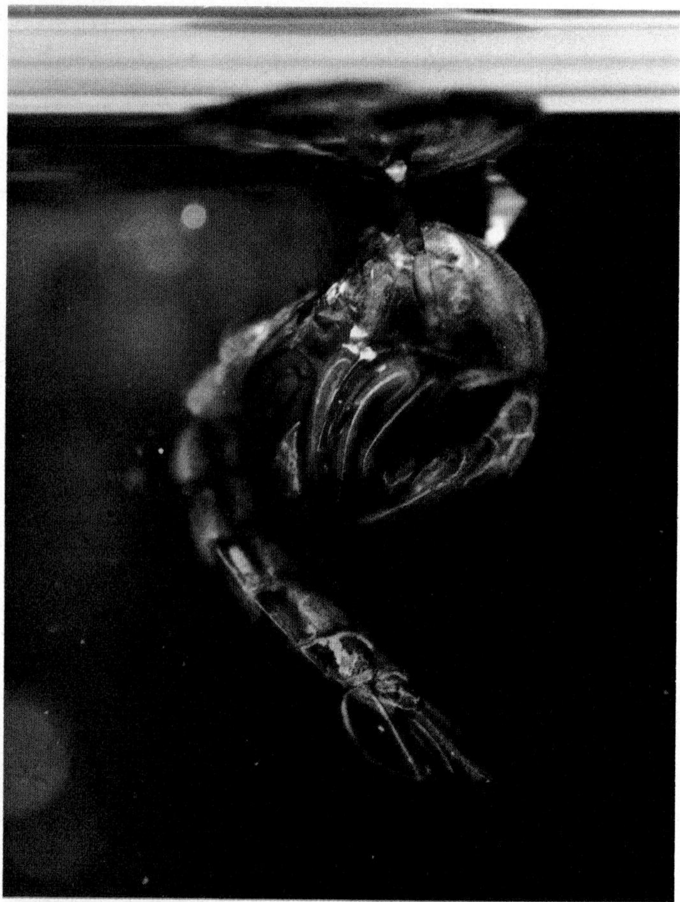

A salt-marsh mosquito pupa floats beneath the surface of a pool.

Shedding its pupal skin, the mosquito drags itself out into the air.

Fully emerged, the salt-marsh mosquito pulls itself onto the surface

until it is fully exposed. Then it swallows air and expands its appendages. Within 10 minutes, its cuticle hardens and the insect buzzes off.

Surviving in a Perilous World

Since most insects spend their entire lives in constant danger of being eaten, over the millennia they have developed numerous ingenious types of protection against predators. The simplest and most common defense is camouflage. For instance, the speckled pattern of the seaside grasshopper *(top, far right)* blends with the natural mottling of the grainy sand, so that passing birds are unlikely to see it. The thornhopper escapes detection by growing a stiff brown cuticle shaped like the thorns on the bushes it frequents.

Another defense is locomotion. If attacked, the thornhopper can quickly leap a foot into the air, unfold a pair of wings and fly off. The grasshopper, too, depends on its ability to jump and flutter out of harm's way. But the greatest leaper of all is the ordinary flea, which can bound 200 times its own length—a feat unrivaled in the entire animal kingdom.

Those insects that lack both agility and disguise have evolved other defense mechanisms. When the larva of the goldenrod leaf beetle is set upon, it can eject from its body a smelly substance that may repel the attacker. And the brilliantly colored cuticles worn by other insects advertise an unsavory taste to potential predators.

Finally, and most simply, many insects avoid capture by hiding; some burrow in the earth, others nestle under the bark of trees, and many restrict activity to the dark of night.

Keeping motionless to avoid attracting attention, a thornhopper feeds on a juicy plant stem.

Everett D. Hendricks, M.D.
1055 Ruth Street
Prescott, Arizona 86301

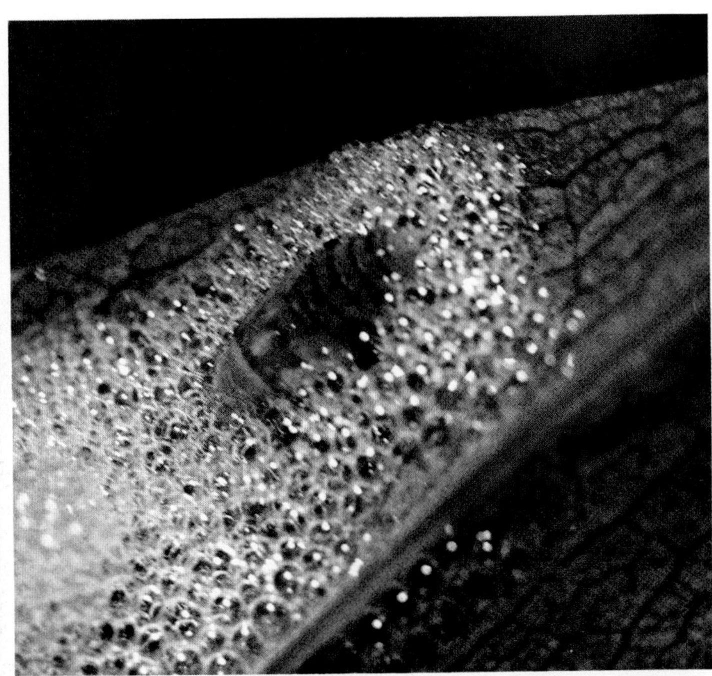

A meadow spittle bug hides under a self-made blanket of bubbles.

The seaside grasshopper can leap and fly distances of up to 30 feet.

A goldenrod-leaf-beetle larva arches up to emit a noxious substance.

The flea beetle's shiny head and back warn of its unpleasant taste.

Protected from some predators by a hard iridescent cuticle, a goldsmith beetle chews its way with powerful jaws through a dogbane leaf.

A goldenrod lace bug uses its long sharp beak to inject enzymes into a leaf. These break down the tissue into a fluid, which the bug then sucks up.

A treehopper draws sap from a stem through its beak. The treehopper, like the goldenrod lace bug, can convert plant tissues to nutritious fluids.

An evening-primrose moth rests on its namesake flower after probing for nectar.

A Host of Voracious Vegetarians

Herbivores make up less than half the number of urban insect species, but it must sometimes seem to plant lovers as though all the bugs in the world were pests. These insects devour leaves and blossoms, chew on roots, bore into trees or wood houses, and drain plant stems.

As their basic equipment, all insects have two pairs of jaws set between an upper and lower lip; however, the shape of the jaws, and their function, vary dramatically. Among beetles, for example, front jaws are used for biting while a back pair holds the severed food. Among other insects—lace bugs, treehoppers and many of their relatives—the two sets of jaws fit together in a slender, sharp tool used to pierce plants and suck their fluids.

In another variation, the back jaws of butterflies and moths are joined to form a long tube, or proboscis, that uncoils from the mouth to draw nectar from deep inside a flower.

Meanwhile, the plants have adapted to the eons-long visitations of insects, and the survival of many plants has become linked with the herbivores' habits. Some 100 million years ago, flowering plants began to produce nectar as a means of attracting insects, which then serve in the process of cross-pollination. When the evening-primrose moth alights on a flower to sip nectar, it picks up pollen on its legs and body and carries it to the next plant. Thus the propagation of its host is assured.

The Deadly Game of Hunting

Insect predators make their living with an arsenal of weapons wielded with a degree of speed, power and guile that the villain in a James Bond movie might envy. For example, the mature half-inch tiger beetle searches for prey by running a remarkably rapid zigzag pattern along the ground. When it sights a potential meal, the beetle pounces upon it and quickly crushes the victim in strong front jaws. In its larval stage, on the other hand, the tiger beetle relies more on deception, hiding in a burrow entrance until some unwary insect happens by; then the larva darts out to make the kill.

Other insects, such as the wasp, kill by injecting the victim with a lethal shot of venom, a mixture of chemicals secreted from a gland in the tail. Some stinging insects, however, merely paralyze prey with venom before devouring it alive or feeding it to their larvae. Still other predators, among them the mature damselfly, trap the intended meal in spiny forelimbs and fly off while the captive is still living to consume it at their leisure.

So overpowering is the feeding instinct that many carnivorous insects —such as the aphid-lion on page 127 —prey on their own kind. Most treacherous of all in this respect is the praying mantis: even when she is engrossed in the act of mating, the female's desire for food is so powerful that she is sometimes stimulated to devour her partner.

A tiger beetle pins an ant larva with one set of jaws; the other rakes the ant into its mouth.

A one-inch damselfly naiad, or aquatic nymph, captures a water boatman near the bottom of a

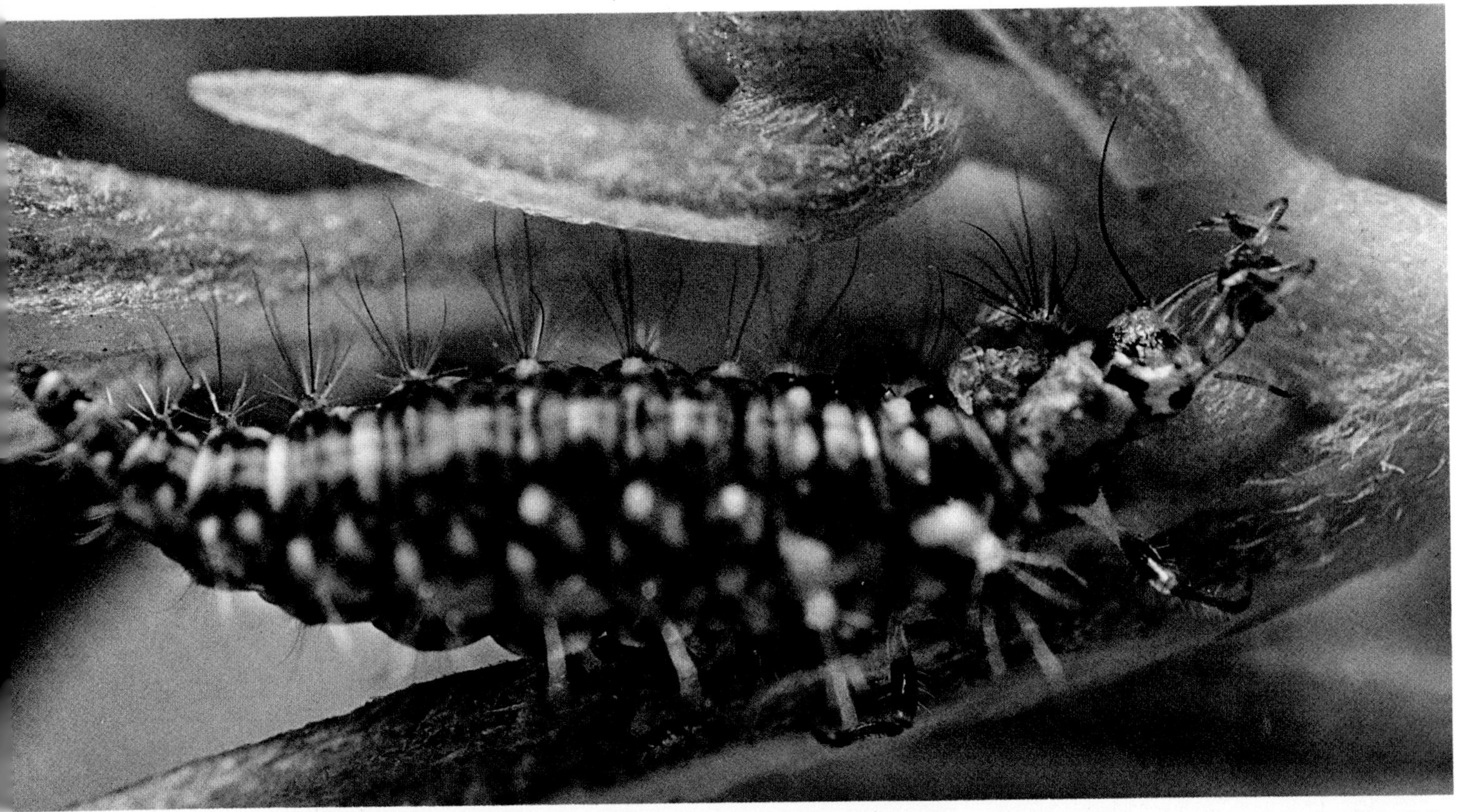

An aphid-lion grips a captive aphid with its long, curved jaws. One of the hungriest of all predators, the lion eats as many as 20 aphids daily.

pond. In seizing its victims, the naiad shoots out its lower lip and skewers the struggling swimmer with the two sharp hooks at the tip.

A praying-mantis nymph clutches a sawfly in its forelimbs as it chews on the victim's head. When hunting, the mantis usually waits at the tip of low vegetation, its spiny front legs raised as if in prayer. When a potential meal approaches, the mantis seizes it with stunning speed, reaching out to its prey in less than 1/20 of a second.

5/ Secrets of the Great Swamp

A town is saved, not more by the righteous men in it than by the woods and swamps that surround it.

HENRY DAVID THOREAU/ *EXCURSIONS*, 1866

To me the most beautiful parts of the urban wilderness around New York are the intricate networks of streams and rivers, ponds and lakes, grassy marshes and wooded swamps that make up the inland wetlands. All too many of the original wetlands have been filled, paved over, built upon or altered by dams in the name of water supply or flood control. Still, precious numbers of them remain. The swamps have a particular fascination; tangled, primitive, darkly enchanting, they beckon like miniature Amazons or pocket Everglades.

One of the largest, about 30 miles due west of Manhattan, is New Jersey's Great Swamp, where green and purple orchids grow among ancient oaks, and mountain laurel explodes into masses of pinkish-white bouquets every June. Ringed by low hills, the swamp lies in a shallow basin seven miles long and three miles wide. The busy towns and highways of the Union's most densely populated state surround it, and only a few years ago it almost became a $220 million jetport. But today the bulk of the swamp—some 6,000 acres of the total of about 7,500 —is a National Wildlife Refuge, and nearly two thirds of that have been set aside as a National Wilderness Area. No buildings, no roads or vehicles are allowed. To see it, you have to get out and walk.

"Bring some old clothes," the refuge manager, David Janes, told me on the telephone when I proposed making a day of it in the swamp. I had been there several times before, sticking mostly to the mile-long boardwalk and observation blinds built to accommodate and channel visitors. But I had not seen the wilder interior. As with most swamps, this would mean a good deal of slogging, with a pair of waders or old sneakers, a can of insect repellent and the company of someone who knew the way in and out.

The weather was dry and not too hot—a fine early summer day. The mosquitoes, which David had warned me cheerfully "can eat you alive" in wetter weather, were few; and those vicious biters, the deerflies, were happily out in less than battalion strength. We parked at a dead-end road on the south edge of the Wilderness Area, where suburban houses gradually give way to old farm fields and finally thick brush.

"This is the old Meyersville Road," David said, pointing beyond a gate that barred all but people on foot. "It used to go to the north side, but we removed the gravel and paving from the roadbed, as well as an old sawmill and a handful of houses along the way, when the area officially became a Wilderness in 1968. As you can see, the road has already grown over pretty well. We planted some rye grass to get things started, but once nature is left alone, it doesn't need much help."

As we walked along the remains of the old roadbed there was ample evidence of the forest's step-by-step return. The sunny fields on either side grew high with flowers, meadow grasses and young shrubs; red campion, blue-eyed grass, buttercups and field daisies sprouted prettily in the path beneath our feet; wild-rose bushes, alders, red maples, young oaks and hickories crowded the sides of the trail.

"You know," said David, "there are so many hundreds of plant species in the swamp that we haven't even finished cataloguing them all. Some of them, incidentally, are edible—like those highbush blueberries over there. They've finished flowering and the fruit is ripening. And we've got blackberries, raspberries, serviceberries, wild strawberries and mulberries.

"The Indians and the early colonists used a lot of other plants, too," he continued, obviously relishing his recital as much as I did. "They gathered smooth sumac and spicebush for lemony flavoring, and the twigs of sweet birch for a very nice tea. They discovered that even cattails are good. The inner stems and roots are tender; some people still eat the young spikes or make pancakes out of the yellow pollen from the catkins, mixed with flour and butter. I'm told they're not bad." David peeled the leaves from a couple of cattail stems and broke off some crisp shoots for us to munch as we walked. They were delicious, tasting like a slightly tart cucumber.

We stopped for a moment, having come to the edge of the true wetland. In a still, shallow pool at our feet, a dully gleaming, brownish-black water snake cruised casually beneath the surface, poking his head up from time to time to look at us. A muskrat splashed away hurriedly through the cattails. As we turned off the old road into the deepening woods, a great blue heron rose slowly from the trees and flew out of sight. David watched it in some excitement; he believed the refuge might be harboring several nesting pairs for the first time this summer, and he was trying to locate them. High in the sky a red-shouldered hawk lazily wheeled in search of prey, uttering its faint *key-yeer.*

The dry ground was disappearing altogether as we entered the meandering drainage of Black Brook, one of four major streams that braid westward through the swamp before joining the Passaic River. David hitched up his waders and I squished along behind him in my sneakers, trying to pick a footing from hummock to hummock by way of the trunks of fallen trees. Green frogs *gunked* from the bulrushes, sometimes fleeing in long-legged panic to plop into the water ahead of us, and big bullfrogs *jug-o-rummed* from unseen haunts.

"There are almost as many different kinds of critters as plants in here," David observed. "We have over two hundred species of birds, and eighteen species of amphibians—counting frogs, toads and salamanders. Great Swamp, in fact, is the only known site in New Jersey for the blue-spotted salamander, which is more often found in Appalachian upland swamps than in wetlands nearer the coast. But you're lucky if you ever see one here because it hides itself so well.

"The same goes for the bog turtle," he went on, ticking off details about the creatures with the same enthusiasm and sure knowledge he had displayed toward the plants. "It grows to be about four inches long, with a bright orange spot behind each eye, and it's one of the rarest turtles in the eastern United States. But we have half a dozen other kinds of turtles, like that one"—he indicated a little painted turtle on a nearby log—"and snappers that run up to thirty and forty pounds. There are a dozen species of snakes, too: brown, garter, black racer, eastern milk snake and some others. None is poisonous, although some people mistake the milk snake for a copperhead and take off in a hurry."

We picked our way along the bank of an old drainage channel dug by settlers long ago to ease their work of cutting and hauling firewood, lumber and marsh hay from the swamp to their farms on the surrounding high ground. David pointed out where refuge crews had shoveled plugs

Everett D. Hendricks, M.D.
Prescott, Arizona 86301

A rain-spattered stream in New Jersey's Great Swamp meanders past mats of aquatic plants and an isolated cluster of drowned oaks.

of earth into the channel at intervals to stop it up and return the swamp to its natural state. In one bank we saw a large woodchuck hole, in another the delicate footprints of a raccoon and a troughlike slide made by a beaver crossing from one stretch of water to the next. Nearby, a beech tree a foot in diameter had been gnawed clean of its bark in a band clear around the trunk. When a tree has its layers of life-giving tissues totally girdled in such fashion it will inevitably die, but this one was still temporarily in full leaf.

"We reintroduced a dozen beaver into the swamp five or six years ago," David explained. "No one had seen any since 1959 and we wanted to have some around. They are mostly bank-denning beaver, but there are a couple of lodges in the marsh area to the north." He moved on ahead, snapping off a huge skunk-cabbage leaf and using it as a switch to discourage deerflies, then demonstrating how it could be used as an umbrella in case of rain.

The terrain in the swamp, I began to realize, was surprisingly varied, changing from wet forest to open meadow to marsh to tiny patches of dry-ground forest in the space of a few hundred yards. This is why Great Swamp supports so many different kinds of plants, which in turn provide food and shelter for so many different kinds of animals.

A male wood duck in New Jersey's Great Swamp peers out from a nesting site in a tree cavity well above the ground. Here the drake's mate can incubate her eggs in relative safety from all predators save tree-climbing raccoons or opossums.

The intricate ecosystem of the swamp had its origin in the last ice age, which ended about 10,000 years ago. The southward-moving ice front stopped just north of where the swamp now lies; as the glacier retreated, its meltwater was hemmed in by mountains—the long fishhook of the Watchungs on the east and south of the present swamp area, and the Ramapos on the north and west. Gradually the meltwater filled up a basin about 10 miles wide and 30 miles long, reaching a depth of 200 feet or more. This lake—dubbed Lake Passaic by geologists—remained for thousands of years, long enough for in-washing streams to deposit 80 feet of clay on the bottom.

But as the ice front continued to retreat farther north, it exposed a gap in the Watchungs; the waters of Lake Passaic flowed out through this opening, carving the roundabout course of the present Passaic River into Newark Bay and thence into the Atlantic. Today little is left of the huge lake but a scattering of marshes and meadowlands that have been nearly obliterated by highways and developments. Great Swamp is the lake's southwestern vestige and the largest of its remnants.

The deposit of clay that underlies the swamp has become hardpan —a subsoil so dense that it is almost waterproof. However, the layers that overlie the clay are anything but. One is peat, made up of decayed plant matter, and the other is muck, a mixture of decaying plant matter and clay brought in by runoff from the upland slopes. Since neither rain nor runoff can penetrate the clay subsoil, they accumulate above it in enough abundance to saturate the peat and muck—thus creating swamp conditions. The peat and muck deposits sprout greenery in profusion, and act as spongy regulators of water flow, reducing the danger of destructive downriver floods. The thick blanket of roots and mud also helps filter pollutants from the water flowing into the swamp.

A third kind of deposit overlying the clay foundation is sand, washed from glacial debris into old Lake Passaic; the lake's wave action piled the sand here and there above the water level, forming islands of drier ridges, some now heavily wooded. As we pushed on through the brush of one such ridge, David remarked that a swamp thicket, while jungle-like, seems impenetrable only to an upright human; down at the level of a raccoon or a beaver there is less of a tangle of branches and a lot more room to move around.

As our walk continued, we came to a stream channel, its water thigh deep. We tested it for a foothold on the muddy bottom, and waded in. David scooped up a handful of the bright green duckweed that covers a good deal of the water surface everywhere in the swamp. This plant, often mistaken for a scum of algae, is among the smallest of the flowering species, producing minuscule greenish blooms in summer. From the duckweed's delicate loose mat of floating leaves—each scarcely an eighth of an inch long—fine filaments of roots trail down, providing housing for all sorts of small organisms.

The water David held cupped in his palms looked tea colored from the tannins leached out of rotting vegetation; and the duckweed in it seemed unremarkable at first glance. Then I took a closer look. Still attached to the plant's trailing roots were tiny bloodworms half an inch long and fresh-water snails no bigger than a pencil eraser. Both of these animals and the plant that harbors them, David informed me, are favorite eating for water birds. By way of instant proof, he dropped his wet handful abruptly to point upstream where the duckweed glinted away into a dark thicket. Seeming not to notice us, a family of wood ducks—a hen, drake and three fuzzy ducklings—paddled around, feeding in the water.

The sight of a male wood duck at fairly close range is always a special event, at least to me. Few artists, if they were asked to design and color a bird, could do a more spectacular job: ruddy, speckled breast, white belly and buff sides, iridescent green-and-purple head with a striped ducktail haircut snappily slicked back, bronzed blue-green wings, set off by black-and-white piping everywhere. Small, shy and graceful, the male wood duck and his more modestly attired mate are almost the trademarks of the swamp. Every March flocks of them begin to wing in from their wintering grounds on the shores of the Carolinas and Georgia and along the Gulf coast.

Their accommodations at Great Swamp are, to say the least, comfortable. To augment the supply of natural nesting cavities in trees, refuge crews have set out about 350 nesting boxes, each atop a long pole equipped with a downward-flaring cone to discourage raccoons, skunks and other animals that like nothing more than to dine on duck eggs. The boxes themselves are the last word in wood-duck housing. Built of exterior plywood or plain mill-run lumber, they are painted a neutral brown or green to blend with the landscape. Most come with either two or four compartments, one per duck couple. Refuge officials have experimented with more units per box, but have found that wood ducks, like tenement dwellers, find the noise and confusion distasteful.

Inside, the floor of each compartment is lined with cedar chips, courtesy of the management; to these the ducks add their own down. When the eggs are hatched, the ducklings discover another convenience. Just below a three-inch hole that has been drilled for use as an entrance and exit, a tiny patch of screening has been nailed to serve as a kind of ladder to help the babies climb out of the nest to the world outside.

The wood ducks at Great Swamp thrive in this luxurious environment. "We have produced about four thousand woodies here this summer," David said with pride. "We call it the Wood Duck Capital of the East. We also have close to five hundred Canada geese in residence, and plenty of mallards, black ducks and teal. We're a major stopping place on the Atlantic flyway; in a good year, we'll be visited by more than one and a half million waterfowl of twenty-two different species of duck and geese."

By now the woodies had spotted us and splashed off around the bend with loud *hoo-eeks*. We climbed out of the stream through a thicket of alder, greenbrier and spicebush and walked along higher, drier ground where maple, oak, beech, shagbark hickory, sassafras and tulip trees formed a dark and handsome glade. David pointed to some matted places on the ground where deer had been resting; suddenly a big buck bolted away through the trees, white tail flashing, and splashed off to safety somewhere in the swamp. The deer population, my companion observed with a trace of sadness, was one of the refuge's big attractions and at the same time one of its greatest problems.

With hunting barred in the refuge, and with no natural predators like wolves or bobcats to help thin out the deer, their numbers had gradually grown to 600 or so, too many to be sustained by the natural food supply. Estimating the optimum carrying capacity of the refuge, officials have figured that ideally there should be no more than 20 deer per square mile. Since the refuge covers about nine square miles, its natural food supply can properly support a total of only 200 deer.

As it is, the animals browse on the swamp's vegetation as high as they can reach, then often wander into the neighboring suburbs in search of food. There they become an expensive nuisance in people's vegetable gardens or get themselves killed on the roads. During the winter, does compete with their own fawns for the browse within reach and many deer die from starvation; not long ago David had counted 10 dead in a single area, and from this he estimated that probably 100 didn't make it through the year.

One year refuge officials decided to try to cull the deer herd by opening the area for a day to 150 qualified hunters—those who demonstrated their marksmanship by specific tests on a target range. Local preservationist groups, citing humane motives, managed to stave off this move by court injunctions for four successive years. "Another try is pending now," David informed me. "I've no idea how it will turn out."

The problem is not the sort that can ever be solved to everyone's satisfaction, and the thought was a sobering one as David and I continued through the forest. Then, suddenly, we were distracted: ahead of us loomed two of the biggest trees I had ever seen. One was a swamp white oak, a species of oak that thrives best in soggy soil. Its immense branches arched up and out with the magnificent display of muscle that, among Eastern trees, only oaks seem to have. High overhead the branches became lost to view in a leafy canopy well over 100 feet above the ground. David and I, embracing the scaly, light-brown trunk from opposite sides, could not begin to touch hands; we figured the tree to be a good 15 feet around and close to 300 years old.

Only 30 yards away stood the other tree: a gargantuan American beech, every bit as tall and broad as the oak, its smooth, steel-gray bole twisting gracefully as it raised its branches skyward. The fact that these trees had escaped the axes of earlier generations seemed a miracle in itself; they were probably just remote enough in the swamp to have been bypassed, and by the time they had begun to approach their present grandeur no man could quite bring himself to cut them down.

The human history of Great Swamp, I learned, goes astonishingly far back, beyond the settlers' efforts at logging and farming. The earliest known evidence of habitation found here is a stone spearhead with a fluted point estimated to be 10,000 to 12,000 years old, unearthed in 1965 by a digging team of the Archaeological Society of New Jersey. This relic indicates that nomadic hunters must have passed through the area, tracking mastodon, caribou or other game adapted to the cold, not too long after the ice had retreated and the plants had recolonized the barren land. On the perimeter of the swamp and inside it, other projectile points and artifacts of more recent origin, some 5,000 years old, have been turned up in dozens of separate digs.

About 1,000 years ago the swamp became a favored hunting ground of the Leni-Lenape, or Delaware, Indians. They were still enjoying its bounty in 1708 when English investors acquired a tract of 30,000 acres in the crown colony of New Jersey, including the swamp. By way of compensation they paid the Delawares the grand sum of £30, plus four pistols, four cutlasses, 15 kettles and a barrel of rum.

Gradually the surrounding land was sold off and in the 1800s settlers moved in on the swamp. Its peat was cut for fuel; charcoal, potash and iron industries flourished on its wood; its trees were fashioned into everything from wagon wheels to ship timbers and railroad ties. In the early 1900s, when the suburbs first began to encroach, the commercial resources of the swamp had been all but exhausted. A few farmers continued to harvest their marsh hay; boys fished in the winding streams and hunters wandered in after coons and deer. During the 1920s the Army Corps of Engineers proposed building a dam that would have turned the swamp into a reservoir, the first of a number of schemes to control flooding of the communities in the Passaic River watershed. Happily, nothing much came of these schemes; but meanwhile the suburban noose continued to tighten. More and more land went for housing subdivisions, and the lowlands adjoining the swamp became a handy repository for garbage and rusting cars.

Then in 1959 came what appeared to be the death stroke. The Port of New York Authority, an agency with a reputation for getting things done, published a study concluding that of 15 sites under consideration for a new metropolitan airport, the only feasible one from the standpoint of cost and accessibility was Great Swamp.

A crab spider, about a half inch long and perfectly camouflaged against flowering Queen Anne's lace, prepares to devour a captive sweat bee. The carnivorous crab spider spins no web to trap its prey; it waits concealed among blossoms to ambush unwary insects that come in search of nectar.

The thought of a 10,000-acre airport with 15,000 workers—not to mention the prospect of jetliners roaring over the sedate communities of Short Hills, Madison, Chatham and the rolling estates of Bernardsville and Gladstone to the west—produced despair and finally plain rage. A Jersey Jetport Site Association was set up to fight the proposed air terminal on the political front. At the same time a Great Swamp Committee was formed to raise funds to acquire land for a wildlife refuge. Housewives in station wagons canvassed door to door and gave slide talks; businessmen buttonholed other businessmen. Within a year enough money had been raised; enabling legislation was passed and land was purchased and turned over to the government to create a federal wildlife refuge. By the time it was officially dedicated in 1964, well over one million dollars had come in from 6,500 individuals and organizations in New Jersey and 28 other states. This was sufficient to preserve nearly 3,000 acres, to which the Department of the Interior has since added another 3,000 acres in acquisitions of its own (it is still picking up parcels around the perimeter, bit by bit).

Today a substantial part of the swamp enjoys legal status not only as a National Wildlife Refuge and National Wilderness Area but also as a federal Natural Landmark, a designation bestowed only upon areas with unique natural features. All this would seem to secure the swamp for centuries to come against depredations by man. David recalled with some relish that when federal surveyors came to chart the boundaries for the new refuge, it took them nearly a year to hack their way through the watery jungle; in mapping other refuges around the country, they said, they had never run into anything quite like this.

Evening was approaching as David and I made our way out of the swamp along a woodland path. A mysterious kind of beauty began to settle over the place; the shadows lengthened through the tangled forest and the sun's slanting rays struck gold on the green-clad ponds.

It seemed a fitting time to ask my companion about certain terrible tales I had heard associated with the swamp: the legend of a swamp devil that is supposed to prey on hunters and berrypickers; of the quicksand that swallows unwary adventurers; of the assorted monsters that go *glonk* in the night. David laughed. "Well, people do get turned around in the swamp, and sometimes they get pretty shaken up.

"You can hear some pretty weird noises in there," he continued; "great horned owls, for example, or barred owls. The barred owl has a loud cry that sounds like *who-hoots-for-you, who-hoots-for-you, ya-all!* That can give you a shiver if you don't know what it is. The barred owl also has an unearthly scream that can sound very much like that of a mountain cat. And it has another call that resembles a faint, drawn-out *hel-l-lp,* kind of trailing off in the mist. That one has even fooled me; once I was about to send a search party into the brush off one of the roads when I finally recognized what it was."

A few months after David's guided tour, I returned to the swamp in somewhat different circumstances. It was winter, and late afternoon. About two weeks earlier a federal judge had finally ruled in favor of a six-day hunting season to thin out the swamp's deer population; the total kill had been 127. But the hunters were gone now, and so were the warm-weather visitors. Heavy clouds threatened rain, and the trees, almost leafless, emerged like phantoms from the receding mists. I set off alone on the boardwalk leading away from the parking lot, stepping carefully to avoid slipping on the slimy planks. The setting seemed like something out of a Hitchcock movie: dank, dripping, ominous.

Yet I realized it was only the time of day and the lighting that made my imagination work this way, for in reality the swamp was as lively and welcoming as ever. As I walked, a mallard paddled off through the drowned roots, a squirrel picked its way across high ground and from tree to tree. After half a mile the boards led me to a delightful pondside blind, constructed on stilts, where visitors could observe, unseen, the swamp's wildlife.

The steps up to the blind are carpeted to ensure silence, and narrow slits are cut in the enclosure so that no camera flash or sudden move can disturb the animals beyond. From here, the sights were a delight. To one side, a squirrel negotiated the branches of a sapling with supreme gymnastic skill. In the pond, blue-winged teals dipped for food. Beyond, on a bank of earth that fringed this part of the swamp, some of the white-tailed deer that had eluded the hunters' guns stood at the edge to drink. They came and went, about a half dozen at a time, seemingly unaffected by the recent shooting. Every few seconds they raised their heads suspiciously, though apparently unaware of being observed. When they finished, they turned and retreated silently into the gathering gloom. I might have been a thousand miles from New York and centuries back in time.

The Round of the Seasons

It is early spring, and New Jersey's Great Swamp is beginning to waken from its winter torpor, as it has every year for millennia.

By the middle of March, buds are opening on trees and flowering plants. The rank, earthy smells of decaying vegetation mix with the fresh, sweet scents of new-blooming blueberry shrubs and spring beauty. As the tender, pale green leaves unfold from their crinkled bud stage, the swamp takes on a bright look of vitality and promise.

In the spring evenings the first chirping of the peepers turns into a chorus, as bullfrogs and green frogs add their rhythmic bass to the alto voices of the barn, screech and great horned owls. During the day a steady hum of wings and constant cacophonous song fill the air, as warblers, thrushes and mockingbirds celebrate their return, establish territories and stake out nesting sites.

In late May, the fragrance of mountain laurel announces the beginnings of summer. A new sound is added: the buzz of hordes of mosquitoes. And as the summer wears on into the dog days of August, only the insects continue their frenetic daily rounds; under the baleful sun, most of the swamp inhabitants quiet down and concentrate on surviving and raising their young.

The days grow shorter, the temperature begins to drop, and the leaves change from their deep summer greens to brilliant reds, yellows and oranges. The birds begin restlessly preparing to leave. The skies become crowded with wood ducks, mallards, Canada geese, flying day after day in apparently haphazard directions. Then, one day, they turn unerringly southward and go.

The first frost usually occurs in Great Swamp at the beginning of October; soon the trees look stark and skeletal against the cold gray skies. Woodchucks are busily eating to store up layers of fat and lining their burrows for hibernation.

When the chill in the morning air lasts all day and the frost on the mud does not thaw out, winter has come to Great Swamp, withering the last green stalks of reeds and marsh grass. Under the surface of the frozen marsh, a few frogs and fish still move about sluggishly. An occasional deer, skunk or raccoon ventures into the open meadows to feed. But mostly the swamp is still and cold, and it seems difficult to imagine that the warmth and bustle of spring will ever return.

New growth on the swamp's edge signals the beginnings of spring. At the base of last year's tall cattails, which have gone to seed, fresh green sprouts are springing up.

Everett D. Hendricks, M.D.
1055 Ruth Street
Prescott, Arizona 86301

An eight-week-old raccoon sits amid grass beaded with early morning dew. Unlike their nocturnal parents, the less cautious young raccoons sometimes roam about during the daylight hours.

Wood ferns (left) thrive at the base of the fungus-flecked trunk of a red maple. These delicate-looking ferns flourish in the dark, humid habitat of the wooded parts of the swamp.

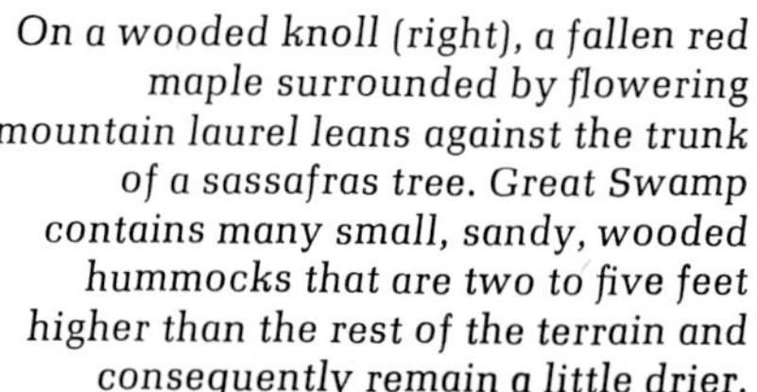

On a wooded knoll (right), a fallen red maple surrounded by flowering mountain laurel leans against the trunk of a sassafras tree. Great Swamp contains many small, sandy, wooded hummocks that are two to five feet higher than the rest of the terrain and consequently remain a little drier.

With the summer sun setting over the swamp, a yearling white-tailed deer comes out to browse on grass near the water's edge. A muddy brown strip between the deer and open water indicates how low the pond's level has fallen in the hot, dry days of midsummer. Pickerelweed and arum grow in the shallows; on the higher land is a stand of oak mixed with cedar.

At dawn in a chilly mid-October, the rising sun illuminates the vibrant color of a red maple. Around the water's edge other swamp hardwoods —oaks, sweet gums and tupelos— are in their autumn raiment. In the left foreground is steeplebush, named for its pointed, spirelike tips.

Flat brown milkweed seeds on airy filaments burst from their pods. The filaments catch the autumn wind and carry the seeds off for germination.

Bright-red nightshade berries droop from a stem. Foul-smelling and poisonous if eaten, the berries remain on the plant after the leaves fall.

Bracket fungus, which sprouts up almost overnight in fall, clings to a cherry tree.

Frost lightly coats the smooth-surfaced, elongated leaves of an evergreen mountain laurel, etching even their most delicate veins in sparkling relief.

On an early December morning, a veil of mist hangs over the swamp. Such mist is common in winter before the ground water freezes; warm moisture from the swamp's surface condenses as it meets the cold air. As the day warms up, the mist blows off.

Ice covers much of the swamp in the aftermath of a winter storm. During ice storms, which occur in Great Swamp three or four times each season, freezing rain instantly coats whatever it hits. Here most of the ice has already been blown off the flexible brown cattails. But it is still clinging to the rushes and hawthorn bushes, which click and crackle in the wind.

Everett D. Hendricks, M.D.

6/ A Backyard Odyssey

There is no need of a faraway fairyland,
for earth is a mystery before us.

WILLIAM T. DAVIS/ *DAYS AFIELD ON STATEN ISLAND*

Early morning in a Connecticut suburb, about 40 miles northeast of Times Square. Through the confusion of a waking dream comes a series of insistent notes—*wheet, wheet, wheet . . . chew, chew, chew, chew, chew!*—like a man impatiently whistling up his dog. It is the cardinal, outside the bedroom window as usual at the unholy hour of 5 a.m., and on this morning in late April he is coming through especially loud and clear. I prop myself up and raise the window shade. The red bird is out of sight in the maple, but down below the house a fantastic picture is taking shape. Through a notch in the dark and greening woods I can see mist pouring up from the pond like steam from a witch's kettle. It billows thickly, higher and higher; the scene might be a stage set from *Macbeth*, a Brazilian jungle, a smoking volcano.

Little by little the air warms and the billows subside into random veils that race across the pond's surface to vanish in a rising breeze. As I watch, the sun slowly breaks above the tree line. The brassy rays strike the water like a cymbal, shattering it into a thousand points of reverberating light.

After such a daybreak, I tell myself, it would be a slothful man indeed who just rolled over and went back to sleep. I pull on some clothes, let in the cat, Whiskers, let out the dog, Sam, and start down to the pond with Sam bounding ahead. Through the bushes I can see a veritable convention on the sparkling water: two tame white ducks the neighbors installed a few weeks ago, plus a half-dozen wild mallards the ducks are showing around. And 12 big Canada geese! I put a hand on Sam's collar and creep up through the brush. Four of the geese are on one side of the pond, paddling around with great dignity and conversing softly with their kin across the way.

The talk becomes more animated, louder; the geese seem restless, ready to pack up and move on. Suddenly one pair sets up an urgent honking, then, beating the water into a chain of white explosions, streaks over the surface to become airborne. The two wheel directly above me, not 20 feet away, wings pumping powerfully, beige bellies glistening, long black necks extended straight as arrows, white cheek patches flashing beneath their eyes. In an instant, the rest of the geese have formed up into a following squadron, booming noisily over me and quickly disappearing beyond the trees. Sam jumps around in sheer excitement and so, to my surprise, do I.

We thread our way into the swampy woods that fringe one side of the pond and find other signals of spring. Along a little stream that wanders there, skunk cabbage thrives, showing the purplish helmets of its flowers and spreading leaves the size of elephant ears. A small crab apple growing wild among the swamp maples flaunts pink buds. A rich display of bracket fungus shelves out from a rotting log in handsome patterns of yellow, brown and white. I snap off a clump of wild-onion leaves and crush it; the scent summons up visions of scallions, chives in vichyssoise and other summertime pleasures to come.

It occurs to me, as Sam and I walk back up to the house for breakfast, that so far it has been an absolutely splendid day. A fine day for taking pictures, too, though I didn't think to bring my camera along. No matter. I recall a famous photographer once saying that a camera is only a device for seeing things, and that some day he would like to take pictures by simply blinking his eyes. Ever since I heard that, I have been blinking or just looking squinty-eyed around me, trying to take everything from close-ups to panoramas without any equipment at all. Besides saving on film and wrong exposures, the technique captures excellent pictures. In the blink of an eye I have seen a milkweed transformed into a design of infinite complexity; an April morning woven into a tapestry of pure delight; a backyard become a wilderness.

Most of us collect pictures that way, I think, whether we use a camera or not, throwing out the bad ones and filing away the good for future use. Those I cherish the most are not pictures of Old Faithful or Niagara Falls, but of things much closer to home.

Backlighted by a rising sun, a thin cloud of mist floats eerily over a pond in the author's backyard miniwilderness.

With a little squinting, for example, I can retrieve images of my backyard in some of its winter moods, with the pond brushed by moonlight and rimmed in snow. The morning after one particularly cold and starry night in December, its surface had changed into the magic of black ice, smooth, dark and incredibly clear except for the blown-glass patterns of air bubbles imprisoned before they could escape. The neighborhood kids, who are not long in appreciating such natural phenomena, were making good use of the ice, skating around in their multicolored mittens and hats like characters out of the Hans Brinker story. Most of the neighborhood dogs were also on hand, running and sliding over the pond in comically splay-legged stops and turns.

Where the stream comes into the pond, the running water, in a semicircle perhaps 30 feet across, had kept the ice from forming. Naturally, one of the dogs fell in, a colossal great Dane named something like Evinrude. He was frantically churning around when I heard the cries of alarm and came running down from the house with a rope. Distracted by fright, Evinrude ignored the rope, so I crawled on my stomach to the crumbling edge of the ice with several pairs of small hands grabbing helpfully at my feet. Abetted by that extra spurt of adrenaline normally reserved for climbers of Mount Everest, I managed to wrestle the creature out of the water and onto the relative safety of the ice. We rescuers then adjourned to our house for cocoa all around, dispatching a shivering Evinrude home with his 13-year-old mistress for a hot bath.

Another December picture in my memory preserves the sharp-edged beauty and devastation of an ice storm, the worst to hit our town in more than 20 years. It started early one morning, after a long night of steady, freezing rain. Like other people who are partial to trees, I cannot bear to watch their trunks and branches being slowly entombed in a heavy coat of ice. In this instance I was spared, being sound asleep, but about 6 a.m. I woke to ominous sounds of tearing and cracking. Almost at once a huge branch hit the roof with a fearful thump, then hung there like a wounded object, miraculously having done no harm. As the wind rose, other brittle, overloaded trees could no longer maintain their ranks and swayed drunkenly against one another, clinking like huge icicles; from time to time one would snap with a sound like the crack of a rifle shot. Three big maples in a row, their roots partly undermined by the stream close by, managed to hold on until one final, fatal gust. They went down together, nobly, with a slow and awesome whoosh.

After the storm, the power lines were in sorry shape too, and we had no light, heat or cooking gas for a couple of days. That first night we lit all the candle stubs we could find, roasted hot dogs in the fireplace, told ghost stories and had a generally good time, going to sleep with most of our clothes on once the last logs had burned down. The next morning, the sun, rising behind the trees, haloed the ice-laden twigs and branches, many of them fractured and dangling. It was a beautiful if harsh tracery, but most of the trees still stood, and they would heal.

Just how vital a tree can be is suggested by one small but striking picture I conjure up of the following spring. My son and I had cleaned up most of the storm damage, awaiting professional tree men for the high-topping jobs. One of our favorite trees, a big shaggy willow, had fared particularly badly because of its brittle wood; its limbs hung down like broken arms. We sawed up all the branches we could reach, stacking the logs outside my study window as firewood for next year.

Working at my desk a month later, I happened to glance out at the woodpile. For a collection of dismembered, dead wood it looked oddly full of life. The willow logs were refusing to call it quits. Trying to keep pace with their parent down by the stream, they were sprouting little green buds and branches all over the place, without any roots or soil to sustain them and only a little morning sun. They kept growing that way for two more weeks, on sheer guts and stored-up energy, before resigning themselves to their fate in the fireplace.

When the sap of spring starts running, a common sight down the road from our house is a row of big sugar maples with taps and buckets attached to their trunks. The tapping is done each year by a couple of young people from the town's nature center, which conducts a remarkable range of activities during the year so school children and adults can learn about the world around them—including how things used to be done by the Indians and Yankee pioneers. All through March the sap drips into the buckets, which are emptied into an old log-fired evaporator in an open shed, filling the air with a faint sugary perfume. It is a slow process, 30 or 40 gallons of sap to make a gallon of syrup. But everyone enjoys it, and the kids even pitch in to split a few pieces of cordwood for the fire. As a reward, they can pour some syrup out, as all New England kids used to do, to make maple taffy in the snow.

Pictures of the past enrich the present. From my window I can see old stone walls crisscrossing the woods, as they still do all over the Northeast. They are another reminder of earlier settlers, who had to pry out the stony gifts of the glaciers, stacking them in fencerows, be-

Willow logs in a woodpile erupt in green shoots, their surviving growth cells stimulated by the increasing light and warmth of spring.

fore they could use the ground for farms. When many of the farms were abandoned for more productive lands to the west, the trees crept back to reclaim the land. Connecticut, for example, was nearly three-quarters cleared for farming by the time of the Civil War; today, despite urbanization, nearly three quarters of the state is wooded again.

The return of the forest, a process called old-field succession, is strangely heartening in this day of the bulldozer and developer, and I chart its slow but steady progress by a series of imaginary time exposures taken just beyond the house. Down by the pond the land is still kept open by mowing, though a variety of weeds and grasses spring up the moment the mower has gone; in a few places sun-loving pioneer trees, mostly small red cedars, have also taken root. Back of the open field, goldenrod and other taller perennials rise in profusion; these, in turn, are being shaded out by thickets of brambles, grapevines and shrubs through whose lush and tangled growth I have to hack a new path to the pond almost every summer. Near the edge of the woods small gray birches and red maples are beginning to take over from the shrubs, and behind them the forest proper is moving in, tall and dense with big maples, hickories and oaks. Only the old stone walls hint that this place was once a clearing where men grew corn or pastured cows.

Such growth and succession may appear somewhat disorderly to suburbanites who like their landscape neat, their gardens geometric and their lawns cut to precisely an inch and a half. But it has a marvelously life-giving effect wherever it is allowed to happen, providing a natural environment far richer than farm land, flower beds or lawns. The wealth of plant foods and hiding places attracts a host of insects, birds, chipmunks, squirrels, woodchucks, raccoons and other animals. They in turn add to the health and animation of the land, putting on a show for the rest of us to enjoy virtually year round.

A male cardinal in full, fiery plumage perches on a tree stump, lured by the prospect of a rich meal of sunflower seeds put out by a suburban homeowner. Encouraged by such easy pickings—often provided throughout the year by bird-watching families—many migratory species abandon their seasonal travels, often remaining north through the winter.

Most of the action in my backyard begins in March, when the ground is beginning to thaw and the sun almost feels warm again. The little black-capped chickadees have been flittering around the bird feeder all winter, using it as a merry-go-round. The blue jays have been in evidence too, elbowing the smaller birds aside and flaunting their handsome colors against the dark tree trunks and snow. But now, with the days lengthening, other birds are becoming more noticeable. Among them are nuthatches, cedar waxwings, mourning doves and a small task force of starlings, who are commuting from somewhere to pick grubs out of the grass.

A pair of bluebirds puts in an appearance earlier than expected and I go down to the meadow to check out the two bluebird boxes I built from an instruction book last year and nailed to a couple of trees. One box, I discover, has had its entrance hole diligently pecked at and enlarged by a pair of hairy woodpeckers that have taken up residence. The other box appears slightly remodeled too, and as I peer into the hole I hear small noises from inside: first a scratching, then a chittering, then a buzzing and drumming. I cautiously unscrew the front of the box and lift it up on its hinge. There, atop a wad of grass and other nesting materials, a pair of white-footed mice stare at me, eyeball to eyeball, as if I had committed some unpardonable sin. Embarrassed at my gross breach of their privacy, I quickly lower and secure the front.

The book that gives you precise measurements and instructions for building bluebird houses also advises you not to be squeamish about evicting squatters when you clean out the boxes in early spring—particularly mice or squirrels, which can easily find homes somewhere else. But I cannot bring myself to rout these particular tenants. I happen to have a sneaking fondness for the white-footed mouse. Also called the deer mouse because of its fawn coloring, it is by far the daintiest and handsomest of its breed. Certainly it is a lot more appealing than the small-eared, pin-eyed, ordinary house mouse that scratches around annoyingly in our wall spaces in the middle of the night.

White-footed mice are named, of course, for the distinctive color of their feet, which oddly resemble tiny human hands; the creatures usually have white bellies as well, which contrast nicely with their brownish-yellow coats. But their most striking characteristics are their large, alert ears and big bright eyes. These features were evolved not for their Disney-like appeal to human observers but for their usefulness to the whitefoot, which is almost entirely nocturnal in its habits and needs to see and hear acutely in order to stay out of harm's way. Its other major strategies for survival, as in the case of many small and unferocious species, are its shyness, nimbleness and sheer fertility; pairs breed regularly through spring, summer and fall, and even in winter if the weather is mild. Young are born in 25 days or less, generally three or four to a litter, and an energetic, well-fed female can produce as many as 10 litters a year.

Nesting sites are an especially urgent concern of the whitefoot, for while these little animals are scrupulously clean regarding themselves, washing and grooming all the time, they can't seem to keep up with their household duties, and their nests regularly get so crammed and so messy that in time they have to abandon those abodes to build others somewhere else. Often a mouse gets a head start on construction by taking over an old squirrel or bird nest—weaving a domed roof of leaves, grass and other oddments on top of it for weathertightness and security—or by moving into a nice cozy bluebird box like mine.

As March warms into April, the tempo of life in our backyard accelerates and there is a decided rise in the decibel rating. Various warblers set up their inanely cheerful singing. A big pileated woodpecker hammers away at a tall tree stump like a pneumatic drill; usually a rare and wary bird, it shows up increasingly wherever the maturing forest has provided large dead trees full of insects and potential nesting holes. Down in the thicket the call of a male ring-necked pheasant resounds like two sharp notes on a toy trumpet; Sam, nosing around, suddenly flushes the bird in an explosion of beating wings.

Along with the new sounds there are bright new splashes of color. A rose-breasted grosbeak swoops in to dine at the feeder, attired in formal black and white with a red bib; later a tiny black-and-yellow goldfinch takes his place at the trough, then darts away in his bouncing roller-coaster flight. The showiest of all is the male cardinal. Even if his alarm clock goes off earlier than mine, it is hard to dislike a bird that has a coat of such brilliant, uncompromising red, possesses a repertoire of clearly whistled songs, eats pesky insects and acts like a gallant gentleman to boot. The female of the species, though softer colored with brown-and-olive tints, is far better dressed than a lot of wifely drudges among birds, and is a no less accomplished singer than her mate. Occasionally the pair join in duets right out of a Sigmund Romberg operetta. No gluttons at the bird feeder, they wisely wait until the big blue jays have stuffed themselves and left before flying in for their favorite sunflower seeds. Sometimes the male hops over to pop a seed into the female's beak. Call it instinct or programed genetic behavior or whatever you like, it looks like a kiss to me.

An impressive number of bird species have begun to make suburban backyards their seasonal stopping places or even permanent homes, finding cover and food in natural and planted landscaping and in the millions of tons of birdseed and suet put out for them every year. The cardinal, for example, used to keep pretty much to Southern magnolia gardens. Over the last 50 years it has extended its range so spectacularly that it is now seen as far north as Vermont, and has become the official bird of no less than seven Eastern states.

Everett D. Hendricks, M.D.
1055 Ruth Street
Prescott, Arizona 86301

Guarded by their watchful parents, four Canada geese about eight weeks old bask at a pond's edge in a suburban Connecticut town.

Even the Canada goose, once so elusive, has become almost a fixture on the suburban scene. Largely as a result of wise management by conservationists—as well as the goose's own adaptability—it has flourished and is now a familiar sight around municipal parks, golf courses, lakes, reservoirs and wherever else there is water, including a growing number of backyard ponds like ours. On their migratory flights from the Carolina coast to places as far away as Newfoundland, the geese work their way north in leisurely fashion, stopping here and there to rest and feed on water plants, grains and grasses, usually arriving at their northern breeding grounds in robust health.

But there also is another side to the story, in which the suburban environment figures as something of a villain. Some of the geese like living in suburbia so well they discontinue their flights and settle down, adding to their natural diet such unnourishing if not downright bloating fare as bread crumbs, pizza crusts and other offerings from well-meaning folk who are flattered to have them around. The result can be a flock of panhandlers, dependent on a chance food supply, subject to malnutrition and disease, and rapidly losing their wariness of hunters as well as their instincts to migrate and breed.

In some suburban towns these big, handsome birds—a symbol of wildness and far-off places—have become so much of a domestic nuisance that park managers have tried everything short of mayhem to drive at least some of them away. One nearby New York state town, I am told, hit on the idea of using the recorded call of a natural predator of the goose, the fox. But the vibrations of this call, so the story goes, had an unexpected result: local police were soon busy on the phone with citizens who complained that their dental fillings were humming. Fortunately, the geese were on the same frequency: they got the message of the fox, and most left town before the populace went berserk.

With this cautionary tale in mind, I have been keeping a close eye on our own town park, where a good 60 honkers now spend the summer in and around the pond. This spring a few broods of goslings were locally produced and made front-page news; photographs of proud parents, with four or five offspring all swimming along in a line, appeared in our town paper. Though I must agree they made a pretty family picture, I hope that most of the geese will heed the traditional call of the wild before things get out of hand.

Sometimes nature moves to thin out the resident goose population by pitting the most vulnerable of them against a predator even more effective than the fox. I like to keep tabs on the size of the families of geese, as well as of ducks, that congregate in our pond, and every so often I notice that a gosling or duckling is missing. Almost surely, it has been the victim of another pond denizen—the terrible-tempered common snapping turtle. Theoretically, the swimming agility of a gosling or duckling should give it a head start over this lumbering foe, the legendary epitome of slow motion. But the legend is partly false: the snapper can swim in stealthy silence and strike with astonishing speed. It steals up on its prey from below the pond's surface, shoots out its long neck, seizes the victim between its powerful hooked jaws, then carries it to the muddy bottom to digest at leisure.

The snapper's death-dealing tactics vary depending on the prey. Fish and frogs—also prized items in its diet—are devoured right at the water's surface. For more substantial targets the snapper reserves a different fate. Two of its most potent enemies are the skunk and the raccoon, which often raid the nest the turtle digs in soft soil near the pond and eat the eggs. If either animal comes close enough to the pond's edge, the turtle pounces, drags it into the water, then holds it below the surface long enough to drown it. Not until then does the feasting begin.

The presence in suburbia of a direct descendant of the age of reptiles, which ended some 65 million years ago, is a paradox both fascinating and chilling. Nobody much likes the snapper; irate bird lovers make periodic attempts to dislodge it, and many people are repelled by its vicious mien, by the powerful heft of the adult, and by its long, scaly, alligator-like tail. On the other hand, the snapper is a link with the earth's primeval wilderness, a symbol of what used to be, worthy of the respect one should accord a senior citizen. For all we know, the species may outlast us; certainly it shows no sign of dying out.

If suburbia suits *Chelydra serpentina*, the snapper, I for one am delighted. I like to visualize a future in which my children will go forth into their own backyards, and all through the urban wilds. And I like to think that they will find an increasing, not a diminishing, number of openings in the dense fabric of humanity through which they can glimpse the real wonders of a world not built by man. It is a priceless world, and it is much too good a show to miss.

An Artful Eye on the City's Byways

PHOTOGRAPHS BY JOHN CHANG McCURDY

By any standards the eyes of photographer John Chang McCurdy are extraordinary. When he looks into nature his vision is that of an Oriental scholar—which he is. And when he focuses his camera, the result—as in the scenes of urban wilderness that unfold on the following pages—is a series of pictures reminiscent of the images on antique Chinese and Japanese silk-screens.

That John Chang McCurdy sees at all is a special kind of miracle. As a boy of 10 in war-torn Korea, he was buried—entombed, he thought—by an American bomb; the explosion killed his parents and nearly cost him his eyesight. Fortunately, the youngster and his extraordinary perception survived intact. Subsequently he was adopted by an American couple and reared in California. There he became an ardent student of photography, and before long began to interpret on film what he saw and felt about the world around him.

When McCurdy set out to record his impressions of the islands of surviving wilderness in and around New York City, he acted not only in his usual role of a uniquely talented photographer, but also as a devotee of wild things. He strolled in Central Park *(right)*, walked for hours on nearby beaches, tramped through suburban woodlands, and drove to the eastern reaches of the grassy fields and marshes bordering Long Island Sound *(pages 178-179)*.

At each spot he sought out the special quality that best conveyed to him the spirit of the place, the time of day and the season. The images that McCurdy's eye and camera picked from these experiences within the urban wilds became a portfolio of places that all city dwellers can find close at hand, when they take the time to learn what to look for and how to see it.

FALL FOLIAGE IN CENTRAL PARK

FLOWERING DOGWOOD NEAR TEATOWN, NEW YORK

FALL-DRIED BAYBERRY AND CORDGRASS AT GILGO BEACH, LONG ISLAND

CRAG RISING FROM THE HUDSON HIGHLANDS

RUSSET GRASSES AND CEDARS CROWN A JERSEY HILLSIDE

Everett D. Hendricks, M.D.
1055 Ruth Street
Prescott, Arizona 86301

WOODLAND GROWTH ON A SNOWY SLOPE 35 MILES FROM NEW YORK CITY

PALE TONES OF EARLY SPRING IN A CONNECTICUT WOOD

EBB TIDE ON LONG ISLAND SOUND

REFLECTED SAPLINGS AND A CONFETTI OF LEAVES IN A CONNECTICUT SWAMP

CATTAILS AND MARSH GRASS AT THE SEA'S EDGE

Bibliography

**Also available in paperback.*
†Available in paperback only.

Amos, William H., *The Life of the Pond.* McGraw-Hill Book Company, 1967.

Barlow, Elizabeth, *The Forests and Wetlands of New York City.* Little, Brown & Company, 1971.

Bent, Arthur Cleveland, *Life Histories of North American Birds of Prey.* Dover Publications, 1958.

†Bolton, Reginald Pelham, *Inwood Hill Park on the Island of Manhattan.* Dyckman Institute.

*Borland, Hal, *Beyond Your Doorstep.* Alfred A. Knopf, 1962.

*Borror, Donald J., and Richard E. White, *A Field Guide to the Insects of America North of Mexico.* Houghton Mifflin Company, 1970.

Boyle, Robert H., *The Hudson River.* W. W. Norton, 1969.

*Brockman, C. Frank, *Trees of North America.* Golden Press, 1968.

Brues, Charles T., *Insect Dietary.* Harvard University Press, 1946.

Bull, John, *Birds of the New York Area.* Harper & Row, Publishers, 1964.

Burt, William Henry, and Richard P. Grossenheider, *A Field Guide to the Mammals.* Houghton Mifflin Company, 1964.

Caras, Roger A., *North American Mammals.* Meredith Press, 1967.

†Cornell Laboratory of Ornithology, *Enjoying Birds around New York City.* Houghton Mifflin Company, 1966.

Cruickshank, Allan D., *Birds around New York City.* The American Museum of Natural History, 1942.

Federal Writers' Project of the Works Progress Administration in New York City, *New York City Guide.* Random House, 1970.

Gertsch, Willis J., *American Spiders.* D. Van Nostrand Company, 1949.

Gilliard, E. Thomas, *Living Birds of the World.* Doubleday & Company, 1958.

Grimm, William Carey, *The Book of Trees.* The Stackpole Company, 1962.

Hamilton, William J., Jr., *The Mammals of Eastern United States.* Hafner Publishing Company, 1963.

†Heintzelman, Donald S., *A Guide to Northeastern Hawk Watching.* Lambertville, New Jersey, privately published, 1972.

Hitchcock, A. S., *Manual of the Grasses of the United States,* Vol. I. Dover Publications, 1971.

House, Homer D., *Wild Flowers.* Macmillan Publishing Company, 1974.

†Kalmbacher, George, and M. M. Graff, *Tree Trails in Prospect Park.* Greensward Foundation, 1968.

Kieran, John, *An Introduction to Trees.* Hanover House, 1954.

Kieran, John, *An Introduction to Wild Flowers.* Doubleday & Company, 1952.

†Kieran, John, *A Natural History of New York City.* Natural History Press, 1971.

Klots, Alexander B. and Elsie B., *Living Insects of the World.* Doubleday & Company, 1959.

The Larousse Encyclopedia of Animal Life. McGraw-Hill Book Company, 1967.

Martin, Alexander C., *Weeds.* Golden Press, 1973.

Moldenke, Harold N., *American Wild Flowers.* D. Van Nostrand Company, 1949.

†New York-New Jersey Trail Conference and The American Geographical Society, *New York Walk Book,* 4th ed. Natural History Press, 1971.

Niering, William A., *The Life of the Marsh.* McGraw-Hill Book Company, 1967.

Orr, Robert T., *Mammals of North America.* Doubleday & Company, 1971.

Peattie, Donald Culross, *A Natural History of Trees of Eastern and Central North America,* 2nd ed. Houghton Mifflin Company, 1966.

*Peterson, Roger Tory, *A Field Guide to the Birds.* Houghton Mifflin Company, 1968.

*Peterson, Roger Tory, and Margaret McKenny, *A Field Guide to Wildflowers of Northeastern and North-Central North America.* Houghton Mifflin Company, 1968.

*Petrides, George A., *A Field Guide to Trees and Shrubs.* Houghton Mifflin Company, 1973.

†Reed, Henry Hope, and Sophia Duckworth, *Central Park: A History and Guide.* Clarkson N. Potter, 1972.

Robbins, Chandler S., Bertel Bruun and Herbert S. Zim, *Birds of North America.* Golden Press, 1966.

Robichaud, Beryl, and Murray F. Buell, *Vegetation of New Jersey: A Study of Landscape Diversity.* Rutgers University Press, 1973.

Rublowsky, John, *Nature in the City.* Basic Books, 1967.

Russell, Helen Ross, *City Critters.* Meredith Press, 1969.

Schuberth, Christopher J., *The Geology of New York City and Environs.* Natural History Press, 1968.

†Wyckoff, Jerome, *Rock Scenery of the Hudson Highlands and Palisades.* Adirondack Mountain Club, 1971.

Periodicals and Bulletins

Cunningham, John T., "A Place to Look, a Time to Listen: The Great Swamp of New Jersey." *Audubon,* March 1969.

"Flora and Fauna of the Great Swamp." Great Swamp Outdoor Education Center, Chatham, New Jersey.

†Heintzelman, Donald S., *The Hawks of New Jersey.* Bulletin 13, New Jersey State Museum, December 1970.

Palisades Interstate Park Commission, "60 Years of Park Cooperation: N.Y.-N.J." 1960.

Skinner, Alanson, "The Indians of Manhattan Island and Vicinity." Guide Leaflet Series No. 41, 4th ed., The American Museum of Natural History.

Acknowledgments

The author and editors of this book are particularly indebted to Sidney S. Horenstein, Department of Invertebrate Paleontology, The American Museum of Natural History, New York City. They also wish to thank the following individuals and institutions. In Connecticut: Mr. and Mrs. Anthony Anable, The Mianus River Gorge Conservation Committee of the Nature Conservancy, Stamford; Ernest Brooks, Albert Kappel and Sam Tanner, New Canaan; George R. Stephens, The Connecticut Agricultural Experiment Station, New Haven. In New York: Warren Balgooyen, Teatown Lake Reservation of Brooklyn Botanic Garden, Ossining; Nash Castro and John C. Orth, Palisades Interstate Park Commission, Bear Mountain; George C. Eickwort, Associate Professor of Entomology, Cornell University, Ithaca; Herbert Johnson, Rocky Point; Samuel S. Ristich, Boyce Thompson Institute for Plant Research, Yonkers; Alex Shoumatoff, Marsh Memorial Sanctuary, Bedford; Nicholas A. Shoumatoff, Trailside Nature Museum, Ward Pound Ridge Reservation, Cross River. In New York City: Albert Baragwanath, Senior Curator, Museum of the City of New York; Andrew Bihun Jr., Roland C. Clement, Richard L. Plunkett, and Roxanna Sayre, National Audubon Society; Donald Bruning, Associate Curator of Ornithology, and James G. Doherty, Associate Curator of Mammalogy, New York Zoological Park; John Bull, Field Associate of Ornithology, The American Museum of Natural History; John Troy Lissimore and Robert F. Mahoney, Gateway National Recreation Area; Joseph F. Melston, Director of Conservation and Environmental Education, New York City Department of Parks; Larry G. Pardue, Plant Information Officer, New York Botanical Garden; Sheldon Pollack, Director of Information, Regional Plan Association; Richard H. Pough, President, Natural Area Council; Natasha Spearman, Librarian, The Staten Island Institute of Arts and Sciences; Frederick A. Szarka, Jamaica Bay Wildlife Refuge; George M. Zoebelein, President, New York-New Jersey Trail Conference. In New Jersey: Catherine T. Bradshaw, New Jersey Conservation Foundation, Morristown; George E. Gage, Refuge Manager, Great Swamp National Wildlife Refuge, Basking Ridge; Barbara B. Hoskins, Librarian, Joint Free Public Library of Morristown and Morris Township, Morristown; Herbert C. Kraft, Professor of Anthropology, Seton Hall University, South Orange; Stiles Thomas, Director, Hook Mountain Hawk Study, Allendale. Also, Roland Eisenbeis, Forest Preserve District of Cook County, Illinois; Elm Research Institute, Harrisville, New Hampshire; David E. Janes, Refuge Manager, Eastern Neck National Wildlife Refuge, Rockhall, Maryland; Martin Litton, Portola Valley, California; Jon Paynter, Indiana Dunes National Lakeshore, Chesterton, Indiana.

Picture Credits

Sources for the pictures in this book are shown below. Credits for pictures from left to right are separated by semicolons; from top to bottom by dashes.

Cover–John Waldvogel. End papers 2, 3–Scott Mlyn. End paper 4, page 1–Kit Luce. 2, 3–John Waldvogel. 4, 5–Ruth Orkin. 6, 7–Arthur Swoger. 8, 9–Kit Luce. 10, 11–Arthur Swoger. 12, 13 –Robert Walch. 18, 19–Maps supplied by Hunting Surveys Limited. 22–Hana Ginzbarg; Paul G. Wiegman–Courtesy Stone Mt. Park, Georgia; Joel Snyder. 23–Geoffrey Gove from Photo Trends; Dick Powers from DeWys, Inc.–D. C. Lowe; Everett C. Johnson from DeWys, Inc. 27–Arthur Swoger. 29–Thomas W. Martin from Rapho Guillumette. 30, 31–Arthur Swoger; Thomas W. Martin from Rapho Guillumette; Sidney Bahrt; Thomas W. Martin from Rapho Guillumette–Sidney Bahrt; Sidney Bahrt; Arthur Swoger; Allen Rokach. 35 through 45–Ralph Weiss. 48–Arthur Swoger. 50, 51–George Silk. 55 –George Silk. 59–George Silk. 60, 61 –George Silk–Thomas W. Martin from Rapho Guillumette; George Silk. 62 through 65–George Silk. 66, 67 –George Silk; William D. Griffin –Allen Rokach; William D. Griffin. 68, 69–George Silk. 73–Sidney Horenstein. 74–Ogden Tanner. 77–Cornelius Mead. 78–"Cheyenne" John E. Bode. 82 through 93–Robert Walch. 96 –Sidney Horenstein. 99–E. R. Degginger; Arthur Swoger–Arthur Swoger; Marjorie Pickens–Marjorie Pickens; Thomas W. Martin from Rapho Guillumette. 102–William Vandivert. 104–William Vandivert. 107–Ogden Tanner; Ogden Tanner–Arthur Swoger; Ogden Tanner; Ogden Tanner–Arthur Swoger; Ogden Tanner. 108–The Bettmann Archive. 111–Sidney Horenstein. 115 through 129–Henry Groskinsky. 132, 133–George Haling. 134 –Leonard Lee Rue III from Monkmeyer Press Photo Service. 139–Henry Groskinsky. 143 through 147–George Haling. 148 through 153–R. G. Schonbeck. 156–Robert Walch. 159–Robert Walch. 160–Ogden Tanner. 163–Ogden Tanner. 167 through 179–John Chang McCurdy.

Index

Numerals in italics indicate a photograph or drawing of the subject mentioned.

Everett D. Hendricks, M.D.
1[illegible]5 Ruth Street
Prescott, Arizona 86301

Everett D. Hendricks, M.D.
10[illegible]5 Ruth Street
Prescott, Arizona 86301